MY
SPIRIT
HELPERS

To: Jon,
A very spiritual lady that has
much to offer.

Many Blessing

Judith Pleasant

MY
SPIRIT
HELPERS

by

Judith Pleasant

BootSun Publishing - Toledo, Ohio U.S.A.

Published by BootSun Publishing
P.O. Box 13139 Toledo, Ohio U.S.A.

You may contact the author or order copies of this book through -
BootSun Publishing - P. O. 13139 Toledo, Ohio 43613

First Publication October 1998

Printed by Corporate Press
Toledo, Ohio

Library of Congress Catalog Card Number: 98-93410

ISBN number 0-9666446-0-3

All of the stories in this book are true and actual events. I have
changed some of the names to protect the privacy of the people
involved. Any name or story that resembles anyone living or dead,
other than the persons or places that were involved is purely
coincidence.

Cover designed by Victoria Gies

Edited by Victoria Gies and Patricia DeSandro

Special Thanks

I would like to thank some wonderful people who had enough faith in me to help sponsor the publishing of this book.

Ankenbrandt Plumbing - Dennis Ankenbrandt owner, who is the best bathroom remodeler that I know, and he has great rates.   He turned our bathroom into a gorgeous sight.
6031 Pickard Dr. Toledo, Ohio 43613 -   419-472-4912

Healing Arts Center - Bill and Phyllis Schnell owners, who give great massages.
3247 Astor Ave. Toledo, Ohio 43614 - 419-382-4267

Royal Pizza - Steve Lang owner, who is a kind young man that grew up with my daughter, and just happens to make and sell great pizza.
4843 N. Detroit Ave. Toledo, Ohio 43612   419-478-8101

Granger Automotive - Don and Pat Granger owners. They are nice people who sell very good used cars, do great bodywork, and have reliable towing.
329 1st. St. Toledo Ohio 43605 - 419- 691-2962

Bassett's Health Food - Joe and Pat Bassett owners. They are very helpful people who are knowledgeable in the health food field, and know what herbs or supplements that are helpful for any ailments.
3301 W. Central Ave. Toledo, Ohio 43610 419-531-0334

My handsome husband Bob, who was generous, and came through for me when it was important to me.

Erwin, a very nice man who has been very helpful, kind, and generous, when a friend needed his support.

AAA Auto Glass – Larry Hutton owner, a very pleasant man that is good hearted, likes Astrology and is quite the business man with all of his endeavors.
210 First St. Toledo, Ohio 43605 -   419- 693-3803

North Towne Flowers – Shelley Deiley owner, a very accommodating lady who gives people their money's worth with the excellent floral arrangements that she makes for all occasions.
5742 Telegraph Rd. Toledo, Ohio 43612 - 419-478-7078

King Ink - KMBS Internet Service - Cary King owner, a nice man who has been very helpful, and is also well priced with recycled ink cartridges and Internet services.
586 Woodville Rd. Toledo, Ohio 43605 – 419-698-1333

Corporate Press – Mark Keesey owner, a cheerful man who went out his way to be helpful and to give me the best price in town on this print job. I am sure his work will make us both proud.   Thanks Aggie
3126 W. Sylvania Ave. Toledo, Ohio 43613
419-473-9555

Acknowledgments

I would like to thank some people who have made it possible for me to write this book.

First, Jim Johnson, a good friend, who was kind enough to help me with my computer, so I could use it for writing.

Don Anderson, a brotherly friend, and my computer genius that has taught me a lot, and who helped me find my book when I lost it in the computer.

My friend, Mona Eppstein, who makes me laugh and was the first person to introduce Sun Sign astrology to me.

Geri Whiting, who has been like a mother to me, and who got me started in Psychic work.

My Sisters, Brothers, other Family members, and Friends, who have gone out of their way to be supportive, although they sometimes don't completely understand what my work is all about.

My husband, Bob, who is not a complete believer, but has stood by me.

My mother, Lucy, who left me some of her ability, and my father, Roy, who always lovingly, called me his Baby.

My clients, for being a part of my learning process. Also for letting me use their stories in my writings.

My friend Patricia, for her encouragement, and help with the editing.

Most of all, my love and appreciation for my lovely daughter Vicki, who has given me her love and encouragement, and gave me faith that I could do it. Also for helping with the editing, and designing the cover.

Much appreciation to my Spirit Guides, for helping with my development.

I dedicate this book in loving memory, to my wonderful mother, Lucy, who always made me feel very special.

Much love and appreciation to Boots, our cat, which has been my constant companion and friend in the natural World and my Spirit Helper in the Spiritual World. Also, who made me feel never completely alone, and always let me know that she loved me.

CONTENTS

TO THE READER -

I think the main purpose that I had for writing this book was to help people to understand that Psychics are just as human as the next person. Sometimes, I think people don't understand that I have the same feelings and have to deal with the same everyday problems as anyone else. I just have a little more confidence in my ability to look at things more clearly to sort things out. I am not tuned in at all times, like some people think, and I do the same everyday things as everyone else. I have hard times and easy times. I feel lonely and sad, happy and proud. I cry tears, and I laugh hardily. I feel anger and pain. I feel love. I have unhealthy times, and I have healthy times. Sometimes material things are important to me, and sometimes they are not. Sharing with friends and family is something that I like to do. My home, family, and animals are very important to me. These are things that are a part of most people's lives, the only difference is, I have a gift that I chose to develop and use in my life for better direction. I hope as you read this book, I will have been allowed to teach you that I am just a regular person, (with Psychic ability.) Some people think that those who possess Psychic ability are evil and of the devil, but I think that is nonsense. Most Psychics are very spiritual people. If they are evil, it's because they have made that choice. When someone questions Psychic ability and whether it is good or evil, I usually recommend that they read the chapter of Corinthians in the Holy Bible. In my opinion, that chapter explains very well about the spiritual gifts that Christ gave us.

INTRODUCTION

There are many outlets for people to use their God given intuitive gifts. Many people don't even realize that they have these gifts, just as I didn't until I was a grown woman.

All through my youth and as I grew up, I had strong feelings about things; I seemed to know things but didn't understand what it was, until I was older and began to explore the Psychic realm. I had to be told that I had a special gift before I realized that I did, but had not been aware of it enough to use it. I think all people are born with Psychic ability and let it go to waste as I did, because they are not aware that it is there for them to develop if they choose to. When I started to work at developing my ability I began to have a better sense about other people and myself. I think it has helped me to be more sensitive to other people's feelings. It has also helped me to sort out people that I choose to be or not be around, because I usually can tell right away if people are good or bad.

Developing my gift surly has given me a lot of direction with my life. I encourage anyone who is interested in intuitive gifts to also develop them, because it can really make a difference in your life, especially if you develop Spiritually at the same time.

Chapter 1

This is the first day of a New Year, and the moon is in Virgo. My sun sign is also in Virgo, so I thought it would be a good time to accomplish some of my goals.

One of these goals, is to write a book about my Psychic work, and some of the strange experiences that I have had since starting to develop my Psychic ability. I would like to start by telling a little about my life, and how I grew up. I hope, by explaining about my background, it will be easier to understand who I am as a person and what makes my work so important to me.

My given name is Judith Pleasant. I don't really know when I started being interested in the Psychic realm. However, as I think back, I guess the interest has always been there, because as a child I remember hearing my mother telling many ghost stories. Although they were scary, they were also very interesting and exciting. Knowing what I know now, I think they were more than just stories. My mother was a very Psychically gifted lady.

I was born in a small coal mining town, named Stonega, Virginia, where my father was a coal miner, and my mother was a homemaker and mother of ten children. I was the youngest of the family. Along with me were seven sisters and two brothers, with our ages about two years apart. Even though we were a large family and our age range was so great, we were a close knit bunch. During those times of my very early childhood things were going well, because Dad was earning money working in the local coal mines. Another reason things were easier then, was because we

1

raised chickens and pigs. We got plenty of eggs from the chickens, and it was very common to see Mom and Dad kill the chickens or hogs for food. The times for slaughtering the hogs were a plentiful time for Mom to make pork every way that she could think of. Along with the pork, always came her mouthwatering biscuits and gravy. I must mention the chicken and dumplings that she made, which were so wonderful, they would melt in your mouth. The corn bread and pinto beans were the best in town.

We also had a vegetable garden, and all of these things were a means of putting food on the table. We had lots of fresh vegetables that came from the garden in the summer, and of course, Mom canned and dried some of them to help feed us through the winter. We had an old horse named Bob that was used to plow the garden. Sometimes my brothers would take me for a ride on him, but I didn't like that too much because it was rough on the bottom. I think they used to ride him back in the hills when they would go hunting for squirrel and rabbits. Mom would cook the wild game and make squirrel and rabbit gravy, and that tasted great poured over crumbled up corn bread. We had many fruit trees, from which we got fruit, such as apples, pears, peaches and paw paws. I spent many hours on the porch helping Mom peel the fruit, so it could be used for baking or canning. Black walnut trees were also there and that's where we used to get walnuts for baking and snacks. Taking the green peel off the walnuts to lay them out to dry in their shell, would make your hands stained brown for days. No matter how much you washed your hands, the stain would not come off until it wore off with time and many washings. There were many bushes around, that were filled with several kinds of berries, that were used for snacks and baking. Mom made great fruit and berry cobblers, lemon meringue pie, applesauce cake, fried

2

apple pies, pineapple upside down cake, and country banana pudding that satisfied our sweet tooth. There were lots of grape vines that produced all of the grapes that we wanted for snacks and making jelly. The grapes were also useful for Dad to make his home made wine. Mom was such a great cook, that we always said she could start with an empty cupboard and whip up a good meal. There was always plenty of food to eat and the necessities of life were a little easier to come by. I have many wonderful memories of that time in my life, of the house where I was born and spent much of my younger life. The old white frame, two story house sat up on a hill they called Buzzard Roost.

Looking down below, you could see a flowing creek that came bursting down from the mountains and through a little gully. The crystal clear water made a wonderful relaxing sound as it made little white peaks while beating against the rocks. The icy cold water continued to rumble down the creek bed as it went beneath a little cross bridge that led to the Baptist Church on the other side of the creek. We made lots of trips over that bridge, and many of them were to go to that little church on Sunday mornings. Behind the Church and across the way, on the other side of the creek were hills and trees that lent beauty to the scene. Over a hill and back a bit farther on the other side, was an old cemetery where the town used to put their own to rest. Between our house and the cemetery was the orchard with the fruit trees that I mentioned earlier. All around us, were the Blue Ridge Mountains, for which that area of Virginia is known. The mountains were so massive and beautiful. They seemed so close that you could almost touch them as they reached up to meet the clouds. The small town sat below them, and they surrounded us with a bluish green beauty that made everyone feel protected from the rest of the world. They still made us feel their peaceful protection, even

3

when they were covered with the mysterious looking fog that commonly crept over them. In the summer time, Mom, Dad, and us kids, spent many evenings sitting out on the front porch, either in the porch swing or in chairs, just being together and talking. Dad always had baseball games on the radio. After the ball game would end, we would sit and listen to the creek flowing; the Whippoorwills, Woodpeckers, Locust, Frogs, Owls, Crickets and all of the other night sounds that you hear in the mountains. It always felt very relaxing and safe. Yet, once in a great while, we could hear a mountain lion in the distance, and that was a little scary, although it stayed in the hills and away from our house. It always seemed a little more scary to hear the mountain lion, after listening intensely to Mom tell her ghost stories, that was a regular part of our nightly family time on the porch. As I think back, I realize how much I really miss that part of my childhood, and all the good memories. Even though, I don't really miss the hard times that were also part of my childhood. As I have gotten older, I realize that was a part of our growing and learning. Although our family was large, as I said before, there was a closeness with us and still is, that you do not see in many families these days. I have had people tell me that they do not get along with their family, and I have a hard time understanding that. We weren't people that showed much affection for each other, but we always knew that there was love in our home. Though we might have had some little disagreements, there was never any hate among us. I think we got along very well, considering there were so many of us. Out of ten kids, none of us were ever in trouble with the law, and with all the rough times that we had to deal with, my Mother knew what she was doing when she was raising us. It is a wonderful feeling to know that even now, if I ever really need anything, my family will always be there for me. I will be there

4

for them as well, and I think that was what got us through.   In the early fifties, when I was still a little girl, the coal mines that my father worked in closed down. It was hard for him to find work anywhere, and that made it hard on our family. When Dad worked in the mines, he only made two dollars a day, but even that small amount back then would stretch a long way, and we got by. After that job was gone, times got really tough. When I say things were tough, I mean, so badly that our electricity got shut off. With Dad unable to find work, there was no money to pay to get the electricity turned back on. We had to use gas lanterns and kerosene lamps for lights. We used a coal heating stove in the front room for heat in the winter. The old house had so many cracks that it was very drafty. In the cold of winter, there would sometimes be ice frozen on the floors upstairs, because there was no heat up there. There was a four burner coal cook stove in the kitchen that we used for cooking our meals and also for heat. Of course there was the outside john that we used. It was so cold in the winter that you only went out to use it when you absolutely had to go. Our baths were taken in a tin wash tub, with water that was heated on the kitchen stove.   There were times, that I remember helping Mom do the laundry, and rubbing my knuckles raw, washing clothes with lye soap on a wash board. Then, we got a ringer washer, and that made doing laundry somewhat easier, rather than so back breaking.

One of my favorite past times in the summer time was swinging on a large vine that was part of a huge old tree. It was on a hill over-hang, down from the house near the hog pens. It's hard to believe that I used to swing out so far over the drop off, since I am afraid of heights. It was probably thirty or so feet to the ground. I clearly remember one day when I was swinging and somehow my hands slipped. I fell to the ground, flat on my back, and though it was a long drop,

5

it did not injure me. When I got up, I felt very frightened, but also very happy that I was not hurt. Someone had surely been looking out for me. We didn't have any bicycles in the family, so I learned to ride on a cousin's bike. Us girls, used to play marbles as often as the boys did, and we were as good at the game as they were. There were also times of playing hop-scotch, jumping rope, and walking on stilts that someone in the family would make. I felt tall and in control, because I was doing something special when I was walking on the stilts. We used to put empty evaporated milk cans on our shoes and walk down the road to make noise on the pavement. There were no sleds for us to play with in the winter, so I used to go sliding down the snow-covered hills on a shovel. Our family learned to be creative, just to have things to play with.

I never was lonely at that time in my life, because there was always someone to play with. Whether it was my sisters, cousins, or my best friend Janice, who was the Doctor's daughter that lived down below us. I also made many friends at school. The school was so small that it only went to the seventh grade, and everyone knew each other, so it was very easy to make friends.

Chapter 2

When I was nine years old, we left the little mining town and moved down to the country. We hoped the move was going to make our lives easier. The house that we moved into was down under a hill, so it was just the opposite of the one we had lived in before. There was a creek across from the house, but it wasn't clean or pretty. Instead, it was green, or muddy when it rained, and didn't make the same flowing sound as the one that we left behind at Buzzard Roost.

It was only a one-story house, and what I remember most about that house was that it had a tin roof. I used to love when it would rain, because it made a wonderful relaxing sound as it fell on the roof. Since then, I have always liked to hear rain fall onto metal, hearing it fall onto an awning, or sitting in a car and hearing it hitting the top. That sound, surely can calm anyone's nerves. The rain falling on the tin roof is the only good thing that I remember about living at that place, other than the fact that it had electricity.

There are some other things that I remember about that place. The most convenient way to get to the house and back out to the main road was through the cemetery. There was another way to get out to the highway, but it was more out of the way than through the cemetery. The graveyard was at the top of the hill, above the house. Us kids used to walk through the cemetery and back again, to get to school or wherever we were going. That would probably make some people nervous, especially children, having to walk through a cemetery every time they went somewhere. It never bothered me to pass through, even when I was alone. Maybe, in some way, I was able to receive messages from the dead even back then, and know there was nothing to fear from the cemetery.

The house was on a farm that we worked for a few years, just so we would have a place to live and could use some vegetables that we grew there for food. Instead of life being easier there as we had hoped, it was harder. There were no chickens and pigs to use as food. There were cattle, but that didn't help us any, because they belonged to the man that owned the farm. I don't think we got paid hardly any money for all the work that was done; and all of us had to pitch in and help. It was supposed to be mostly a share cropper deal, but mostly what we got to share was the work. It was not what it was cracked up to be. People can surly get stuck in bad situations when they are desperate to survive. The hardest part of farming was working out in the fields and taking care of the sugar cane that we grew to use for making molasses. If we didn't loose the cane from rains or wind, then at harvest, we all would get together and make the molasses. We all would take turns stirring it. The molasses was cooked outside over an open fire in a huge trough. Stirring that stuff over and over as it cooked, made your arms feel as though they would fall off. That sure was not one of my favorite things to do as a child, especially, since I hated molasses. However, it was something that had to be done. The little bit of money that was brought in from selling our share was another means of survival. Another thing that brought in a little money, were some herbs that grew wild on the farm. I helped Mom gather them up, and Dad took them someplace to sell, because they were used for medicine. As I recall, it was Echinacea and Ginseng. Yet try as we may, things seemed to keep getting tougher and putting food on the table was harder. There were times that if it wasn't for Mom's biscuits and eggs, us kids would not have had sandwiches for our lunch at school. That was very hard for me. I was embarrassed that we had to use biscuits for our sandwiches, while the other kid's parent's could afford to buy loaf bread from the store. As I think back, that was the most embarrassing thing that happened to me in my childhood.

Unlike the other house, I don't really have very many good memories of that place. What comes to mind is that there were no friends near by to play with, and I was very lonely. I spent many Sunday afternoons on the front porch swinging on a porch swing, and singing songs to myself. The only person that I had to play with, was a little boy that lived up the hill from us. His name was Clifton, and he thought he was my boyfriend, but I knew better because I was too young for boyfriends. He was a nice boy, and so thoughtful that he got me a doll one year for Christmas. He must have realized how poor we were and that the doll would be my only gift. I was shy about taking the doll, but I did, and he was very happy when I accepted it. He was a good friend, but having him around wasn't like having girlfriends to play with. It was sad to feel that my only friend there probably felt sorry for me because we were so poor and had such a bad time trying to survive. It definitely had been a bad choice to move there, and I was glad to leave, even if it did mean saying good-bye to my friend Clifton.

Finally, things got a little better because Dad got a job as the caretaker of a new cemetery that they had just opened. Then, we were able to leave the old farm that was lonely and where there was too much work, to move to a small town near by. We lived in a couple different houses in that town. The last two houses that we lived in had an inside toilet, and a real bathtub. That was when I was around fourteen years old.

Things had definitely eased up somewhat, because Dad was earning money at his job. Some of my sisters cleaned houses, and we baby-sat for people, but it still was not always easy.

I wonder, how many people at my age, can look back and say this was part of their growing up, and feeling that their life shouldn't have been quite so hard. Nevertheless, it builds character. As I said, the love in the family made it all easier to deal with, so that made it all worth while. To be honest, I guess I wouldn't change those things for that reason.

Chapter 3

A few years later, when I was eighteen, our family moved north. Some of my older sisters and brothers that had drifted North earlier to find work talked my Mom and Dad into doing the same. Our move was to Toledo, Ohio. Dad got a job running a gas station that also did repairs, and he made a decent living while working there. It really felt good not having to rake and scrape for food and other of life's necessities that many people take for granted. Making that move was probably the best thing that my parents could have done for me. Although, it might not be my ideal city to live in, it has been good to me.

The hardest thing that I had to deal with after we came here, was my mother's illness and death less than four years after our move. Nevertheless, her death left me with many good memories and lessons about my childhood. At that time, I had no idea how helpful they would be to me later. Mom's passing, made me realize how much I missed her, my best friend. Memories of her take me back, and I realize that the time we had together was precious. Nostalgia from that period of my life brings many thoughts of her and the closeness that we shared. By sharing some of these memories, I hope to make it easier to understand who I am and what I am about. I'm sure that period of my life played a large part in why and how I developed my Psychic ability. Since we were from the South, and had a religious upbringing, anything that had to do with using any Psychic abilities would surely have been kept hidden. So much so, that I don't think even my Father knew about some of Mom's abilities.

She was forty three years old when I was born, so we didn't do many of the things that most mothers and daughters do together. By the time I got old enough to do anything, she was too old to do things with me. So mostly what we did, was sit and talk, listen to the radio, or watch television. We didn't get the TV until I was around twelve years old. We would also play Mom's favorite game, which was Checkers. She loved to play the game, and I can understand why she liked to play it so well. In fact, she was such a whiz at it that I never won, nor did anyone else. I was her baby, but she didn't let me win. She took pride in winning the game, no matter whom she played. The time we spent together was very special, because we became very close. Loving this lady was very easy. She was a very special soft spoken person that everyone loved. I have never heard anyone speak badly of her, and to me, that is quite a legacy. I hope that in some way, she has left me some of her personality as well as her abilities. I would feel truly blessed. Some of her abilities probably came from our Native American background. I wish I had tried to find out more about our heritage while Mom was alive, other than the fact that I know I am at least one fourth American Indian, mostly Cherokee. We also have some Blackfoot and Cree blood. Just by looking at my mother and her mother, they appeared to be Indian squaws. They had a deep olive color and long black hair that they always braided, and sometimes pulled back into a bun.

Some of the things that Mom and I talked about were things I'm sure she hadn't shared with anyone else. I know that she believed in herbal medicine, because I remember some remedies she used to use, such as the horehound and licorice drops. She fed us fried onions for congestion. The fried onions were also used as a poultice that she used to make for Dad and us kids when we had chest colds. (A poultice is a soft, wet, warm, cloth filled with herbs or medicine that is applied to a sore part of the body.) I especially remember the night she died, when she was begging me for a poultice for her painful stomach.

There were many things that she taught me that was helpful. One of those things, is something that I still use for burns, and that is petroleum jelly. If you put it on immediately, it takes the "burn" out and you probably will not get a blister or scar. One time that it worked great was after Mom died. Dad was checking the furnace in the basement, and it blew out in his face. He was burned pretty badly. I happened to be there, and ran for the petroleum jelly to put it on his face and neck. I took him to the doctor, and the doctor told me that I had done the best thing possible. Dad didn't end up with any scars. I was glad that I had remembered one of Mom's remedies. Once, when my daughter Vicki, was two, she pulled a hot iron off of the ironing board onto her face, and it burned her cheek. I put the Vaseline on her face right away, and rushed her to the doctor. Although, she had second and third degree burns, she was left with no scars. Another thing that Mom used to have us use for burns, was to cut a raw potato in half and scrape part of it off and put it on the burn; that also took the "burn out." Of course, the petroleum jelly was a lot less trouble and messy to use, but sometimes you had to use what was available.

There were many things, or sayings that Mom taught me, that most people would call superstitions. Some of these things were:
If your nose itches, someone is coming to your house; the right side means a man; the left side a woman.
If your left palm itches, you are going to receive money; the right palm means your going to get a letter or shake hands with a stranger.
If your upper lip itches, you are going to kiss a fool.

If your ears itch, you will hear news from a man if it's the right ear, and a woman if it's the left.

If your ears burn, someone is thinking or talking about you, right one, a man, left, a woman.

If your left eye itches you will be pleased, right, made angry.

If the bottoms of your feet itch, you will get a new pair of shoes, or walk on strange land. My favorite one, is when the nose itches, I always know when someone is coming to my house, so it is a good warning of company coming.

There was the saying, that when you hear a dog howl, you would hear of a death around you. If a bird or bat flew into your house, there would be a death. If a picture falls off the wall, there would be a death.

Mom gave me a secret remedy on how to remove warts, and it worked, but I'm not going to tell how it is done. I don't feel I can tell anyone about it, since it was her secret that she passed down to me, and the promise that I made to her, to keep it to myself.

She also showed me a way to find out what the person would look like, that you were going to marry. (You need to start with a darkened room, and light a candle, that you set on a dresser. Stand with your back to the dresser mirror, as you look into a glass of water that you hold up by your left shoulder. The reflection from the candle flame, shining into the mirror, is supposed to show a vision of your true love in the glass of water.)

I was too naive to know that most of this stuff that I grew up thinking was normal things that everybody knew, were in fact, special things that most people would know nothing about. Mom had much knowledge to give, had I only been aware enough to accept it.

Chapter 4

Thinking of Mom takes me back to the old house on Buzzard Roost, and the many things that happened there. All of the stories that she used to tell about it being haunted, are as clear in my mind as if it were yesterday. Other people used to tell the same things that Mom did, about some very strange things that went on there. Since so many ghost stories had been told about that old place over the years, at least some of them must be true.

I remember being awakened one night and hearing strange noises upstairs, in the room that they said was the most haunted. We had an old sofa up there and it sounded like a person jumping up and down on it, back and forth from end to end. It woke my mother and most of the other members of the family. It continued to jump until my mother went to the stair door and yelled, "Cut that out up there." The noise stopped immediately, and we never heard it again. We knew there wasn't any family member up there, and it was too much noise for it to be a mouse. So, whatever it was, the sternness of my mother's voice kept it from ever doing that again. I recall, when I would go into that room, I would feel nervous, as though there was some sort of presence there. Other stories were told over the years about that spooky old room. One that comes to mind, is that family members would be able to hear one of the windows raise and it would sound like someone pouring apples into a metal bucket. When it was done, they could hear the window being put back

15

down. It always used the same window, which faced the direction of the old cemetery. My mother had told of the times that she heard what sounded like someone setting a dinner table, and then serving up food. She could also hear the silverware touching the plates and the cups being set on the saucers. She was never able to explain that occurrence, because there was no dinner table up there. Also there were the stories of something dancing on the floor above, and then, it would stop dancing and jump on the bed. After awhile, it would get back down onto the floor and keep dancing again until it was done. I don't recall ever hearing those noises myself, except the couch jumping incident. I heard the couch jumping story told many times by different people. The thing that always caught my attention, was about my mother yelling to it and it stopped, but she never seemed to fear it.

Something was definitely eerie about that room that made everyone who walked into it feel uncomfortable. We had two beds in it, and my brothers, Jimmy and EC slept there in the beginning, before the noises got so bad. I don't recall anyone sleeping in it in later years. Another large room was adjoining that one; we had beds in it that my brothers used after they moved out of the spooky room.

A strange thing happened to my sister June once, that we were never able to explain. One night, when she was fairly young, she woke up with her big toe hurting and bleeding, and my parents had to rush her to the doctor. They checked the bed to see if there was something in it that she could have gotten cut on, but were unable to find anything. To this day, we could never explain the cut, but she still has a scar that looks like a crescent moon on her toe as a reminder of the incident. I was so young when we moved from that house, I really wasn't old enough to understand or to know enough to ask questions. For that reason, I feel I missed out on a lot of information that Mom could have given me. My mother must have had Psychic abilities, because she was always right. If we went against what she told us kids to do, our plans always backfired, and we would get hurt or something. So we soon learned to listen to her and mind what she said.

One of my cousins, named Jenaine that I went back to Virginia to visit reminded me that she used to stay at our old house often. She said, Mom used to read coffee grounds for her and my sister Marg when they were growing up. That made me believe that Mom had more Psychic ability than I had realized before.

I was only twenty one years old when Mom passed. I never dreamed that the information that I thought was so unimportant when I was young, would be so special several years later. I wish, I had known more about the Psychic realm before she passed over to the other side. If I had only known, I would have tried to learn and absorb as much as I could, because I'm sure she had much to teach. It would have been very rewarding, to learn all the information that she could have shared with me.

Chapter 5

After Mom's death, my life became very ordinary. I had met a young man whose name was Jim, shortly before her passing. Jim and I had not known each other very long when we decided to get married. When Mom was very sick, I told her our plans, and her reply was, "I don't know why you want to marry him." I guess she was right again, because Jim and I got married the following year and it wasn't always a happy marriage. Twelve years later, he left me for another woman. I think my dreams were meaningful even back then, because I used to have vivid dreams that my husband was cheating on me, and it turned out, he did just that. (Vivid dreams, are dreams that are very pronounced and foretell future events, and they are called precognitive.)

I did get one good thing out of that bad marriage situation, and that was my daughter Vicki, whom I love very much. After my divorce, she gave me the strength and determination to make it on my own as a single parent for fourteen years. It was a lot of hard work trying to raise an eight-year-old girl by myself, but she cooperated very well and by us working together, she got her college education. She now has a Bachelor's degree, in Fashion Apparel Design. I feel very proud of us, especially her, for making it through. Thank God, a couple of my sisters lived close by to help keep an eye on her when I wasn't home. She has been quite an inspiration to me. I feel that tapping into my Psychic abilities has helped me with her life, as well as keeping my own life together.

Vicki also has some Psychic ability. She has practiced Tarot cards to a small degree and did very well, but she did not get very in depth with them as of yet. I'm sure there will come a time when she will be more interested in them and decide to pursue them further. When this time comes, I will share with her any knowledge that I may have on the subject. She has always seemed older than she was and had a down to earth knowledge of things. I think it is her built in intuition that seems to help her to know what is going on around her. She gets pretty good gut feelings about people and things. I sometimes ask her for intuitive advice when I am too close to a situation to trust my own instints. She definitely has a gift that she uses with an earthy nature. Maybe she inherited some of that from her grandmother Lucy and me.

Chapter 6

I became deeply interested in metaphysical subjects after I separated from my first husband. Right around that time, I met a woman named Mona, and we became very good friends. She had just separated from her husband also. We were two women who had been put out into the real world to learn how to survive on our own, and to raise our children by ourselves. I think some of the fears and problems that we both had to work through made our friendship very strong. We had many ups and downs, shared tears of sadness and of happiness. We grew a lot within ourselves, with each other's help over the years. The friendship we had became so close that we could tell each other anything. She is the person that got me acquainted with Sun Sign Astrology, and that eventually led me into the Psychic field. We would discuss the different personalities of all the signs, and what sign matched what, or what sign didn't. That led me to start buying astrology magazines, and I became more interested in the subject.

Because of that interest, I was talking with a young man named Steve that used to work with me. He told me his mother knew a very good Astrologer. I asked her name, and how to contact her. He told me he would get the information from his mother. Shortly after that, he brought me her name and telephone number that I had requested. I made an appointment and went to see her. Her name was Geri, and she seemed to be a very nice lady. She also seemed to know a lot about Astrology. She did a very in depth natal "birth" chart, which was gave me a lot of details and was extremely interesting but not exactly what I was looking for. I called her about a month later, with disappointment about the chart. She told me, what I wanted was a compatibility chart. She thought I had wanted a natal chart before. She apologized for the misunderstanding, and then did the compatibility. I was very impressed. From that day on, we became good friends. If there was ever a friend that could feel like a mother to me, she was that person. I always felt like I could count on her, like I could my own mother.

We spent a lot of time doing Astrology, and she taught me a lot about the basics of the subject. She had told me, while doing my chart the first time, it showed repeatedly that I had a lot of Psychic ability and a healing hand. One day, after I had known her several months, she gave me a deck of Tarot cards and told me to go home and practice with them. (Tarot cards consist of a deck of seventy-eight cards, with pictures on each card that has several meanings. The study of them, and your Psychic ability, helps you discern the meaning of the cards appropriate for the person you are reading for. These cards have been around for centuries, and are said to have originated in Europe, as a means of predicting the future).

I sometimes wonder why God let me wait until I was in my late thirties to start working toward my Spiritual and Psychic development. At that time, I started practicing with the cards and paying attention to this Psychic ability that Geri said I possessed. I was surprised how much I had that I hadn't even paid attention to before. For example, I would be on my way out to meet my girlfriends, and while driving there, someone would come to mind that I hadn't seen in ages. When I would get to my destination, that person would be there. Things like that became more and more frequent and it was so strong, that I couldn't believe I had not paid attention to it before. I definitely had let my ability go to waste for too long. Some things happened then, that I wasn't completely comfortable with because I didn't know what they meant. Since my development was still new to me, there was a lot that I didn't understand. My father had passed over, and after he did, I dreamed several times of seeing him in his casket. It was as though he did not want to be dead and he kept trying to get out. I would always try to make him stay in the casket and to realize that he was dead. I would wake up really upset, with the feeling that he didn't want to be there. Sometimes, on my day off from work, I would take a nap during the day or would be sleeping at night, and wake up abruptly out of a deep sleep, startled. It seemed as though someone was standing over me watching me sleep. I saw a man's presence, and also a woman. My father, Roy, and my sister, Virginia, who had also passed over, came to mind and I felt that was who they were. I woke up one night, and saw a woman with my sister's features, except she had long hair like mine. (She and I looked a lot alike). She was standing directly over me, and just looking down at me. I was so upset at that moment that I asked God to not let anything like that happen again, and it didn't. After that, I don't recall ever having the dream again about my Dad and the casket either.

I talked to some of my Psychic friends about the figure that kept waking me while standing over me. They said, that it could have been my Spirit form coming back into my body, after an out of body experience and it woke me doing so. (An out of body experience, or astral travel, is when your Spirit leaves your body, and is able to go places, experience things, and then come back to your body again.) It is thought to be the reason for so much deja vu, and feelings of "been there, done that." Well, whatever it was, I'm glad it stopped: it was scary because I couldn't understand or explain it.

It was then, in the first stages of my Psychic development that many incidents began to happen. Since I was just a beginner on the subject, I was surprised at how accurate I was becoming with my predictions. One night, I had gone out to meet my friends. We were at our favorite hangout, listening to the music and talking. I had met a man there, just a few months before. His name was Kurt, and we had become very close friends before he decided to move to Florida. I was really in tuned with him, and I seemed to always know when he would be getting in touch with me. That evening, I was compelled to keep watching the door. My friend Dusty noticed and asked me who I was looking for. I told her that Kurt would be walking through the door at midnight, and much to Dusty's amazement, he did walk in at exactly 12:00.

When he walked up to greet me, he said to me, "You don't even seem surprised to see me."

I said, "I'm not, I knew you were coming."

He said, "'How could you know? I didn't call you and tell you I was in town for a visit because I wanted to surprise you."

I said to him, "I just had a strong feeling that you would be here."

Things like that began to happen more and more frequently, and it started to make me feel that I had a special gift. At the same time, I would feel uncertain as to just how much ability I really had. I guess, that was how I was supposed to feel, because I still do to some extent. That is probably good, because it keeps me on my toes. It makes me realize that although I might be right often, nobody's perfect and right all the time. So, for that reason, it makes me open to the fact that there is always room for learning and improvement. I studied Tarot daily, buying several books, reading, studying, and practicing more. Not only did I buy books about the Tarot, but also about other areas of

Psychic development such as, channeling, Spirit contact, Psychometry, Psychic healing, Spirit guides and other Spiritual subjects.

Matters pertaining to ESP (Extra Sensory Perception) became more and more intriguing to me as I continued to learn.

I went out after work a lot to hang out with my friend Dusty and some other people that we knew. Sometimes I would practice my ability for her by giving her bits of information. Once I told her that I felt she would have a very unexpected sadness in her life. Her father was ill at the time, so she thought it was connected with him. Her father died soon after that.

Six months after he died, her brother had bypass surgery, and although he made it through the surgery, he died that same night. His death was very unexpected, and Dusty was more saddened by that than anything else that had happened in her life.

One day, I called Dusty on the phone, and told her that I was concerned about her because I felt she was having some pain. She thought I meant emotional pain, but I said I thought it was physical, and around her back. She admitted that she had been having some pain with her hip and back.

On another occasion I told her I was very concerned about our friend Kurt. I felt that there was something very wrong with him and it made my heart feel heavy. We found out later that he was very ill and had died without me getting to say good-bye to him. I hadn't been in contact with him for awhile and was very sad when I realized I wasn't able to see him before he died.

I guess everything happens for a reason, and sometimes only God knows what it is. I had a gut feeling that Kurt had passed over, and maybe it was best that I didn't know until after it happened, because I think I would have had a hard time accepting it.

Chapter 7

I had been studying for several years before I was comfortable reading Tarot for anyone except myself. It was a big responsibility to tell people private information about their lives, and I was not sure I was ready for that.

However, it seemed as though everyone else was ready for it, because I worked as a department manager for a large retail chain, and I had friends at work that began to talk me into reading for them.

My first reading for anyone else was for Tracy, who was the sister of one of my fellow employees. Tracy came in to the store one day to see her sister, and while she was there she looked me up and ask if I would do a Tarot reading for her. I was a little nervous, since it was new to me, but I agreed to do the reading. Tracy and I went into my stock room, and I laid out the cards, to do a mini reading for her.

That was the first of many times, for me to sneak back into my stock room and lay out the cards for an associate. In the reading, I saw that she would be having a baby in the immediate future. She thought that was impossible, because she had surgery to prevent having any more children. I repeated, that I saw her having a baby soon.

It was less than a year later, that Tracy let me know I was right. She came in to the store and said that she just had a baby. She was very upset with her doctor and his birth control surgery that didn't work. She felt he was responsible for a birth that she hadn't planned.

Since that, I have found that not only can I foresee pregnancy, but also I do really well at predicting the sex of a baby before hand. In fact, there have been a couple of times that the parents have been told that it was a certain sex, according to an ultra sound taken. I said that it was wrong, and when the baby was born, I was right. There have been many times when people already knew what sex their baby was, and would ask me what it was just to check my accuracy. I was at the Dentist's office one day, and the receptionist, whose name was Jenny, asked me when her daughter in-law was going to get pregnant. I said, "Two, but I was not sure what two meant." When I went back to the Dentist again, Jenny said a couple of days after we had talked, her daughter in-law had miscarried at two months into her pregnancy; and it was twins.

After that, I started to feel a little more comfortable reading for other people. I started giving mini readings for other people at work and that helped to build up my self confidence. The feedback from other people, let me know how I was progressing with my development. There were many of my associates that were interested in my Psychic ability, and willing to let me practice on them. One of these people was a lady named Pam, who worked in the office. She and I had become good friends through the years as we worked together We had both had similar lifestyles, so we had a lot in common, such as, she had an only daughter as I did and we were single Moms. At that time her daughter Becky, was around sixteen years old. One day when I was up in the office, Pam asked me to do a reading for her. As I did, I saw her daughter getting married and having a baby boy before she was nineteen. This was hard for Pam to believe, especially since she had better plans for her daughter, like going to college and pursuing a career. Nevertheless, it all came about exactly as I predicted, and much to Pam's dismay. But she did get a wonderful grandson that she loves dearly to compensate for the other disappointments. I had also made many predictions for Jan, one of the managers that worked with us. She was a super person, even if she was in higher management. She and Pam, would have me come up to the office to read for them. Thank God, the store manager didn't catch us doing readings. The information that I gave Jan turned out to be more accurate than I would have thought. At first, she didn't want anything to do with a reading because she was very Catholic, and felt it would go against her beliefs. As we became better acquainted, we became closer friends. She then felt comfortable enough to ask me to read for her, due to Pam's, encouragement. With the first reading, Jan became fascinated with the Psychic field. Shortly after that, she became so interested that she decided to study Tarot cards. She picked up on them quickly, because she had a lot of Psychic ability. One of the things I predicted for her was, that she was going to get a promotion that would take her back to her hometown. She would have a little boy, and all of those things would happen within a year. She didn't believe the part about the baby, she didn't have time for children then, because she wanted to pursue her career. Within a year, she had a baby boy and was transferred back to Pennsylvania, where she was from. The bosses promoted her to be manager of a store, and from what I hear, she makes a great mother.

The office manager, whose name was Marie, also had me to read for her from time to time. She had a keen interest for tarot cards, and she seemed to think that I was getting pretty good with them as time went on. The most important thing that I remember telling her in a reading, was that she would become pregnant with her partner. She told me that was not likely to happen because he couldn't have children. I told her that she was wrong because he could have children. She kept arguing the point with me, until one day she found out that she was pregnant with his child. She didn't argue anymore with my predictions after that.

When I first started reading, I felt that doing Tarot cards was something I knew I was supposed to be doing. I enjoyed studying and working with them so much. In my spare time, I would sit and work for long periods with my cards, practicing over and over again. I started reading more about Spirit guides, and how to get in touch with them. How to heal yourself and others, and ways to do Psychometry. I tried Psychometry, with no results. (Psychometry, is holding someone's personal item in your hand, and getting Psychic impressions from it, such as pictures and feelings.) I only tried it once and didn't get any information, so I guess it wasn't the right time to put much effort into it. I put it aside and did nothing with it for awhile. I kept getting more involved with my Psychic studies. I felt there were other areas that I wanted to explore, such as, channeling Spirit. I started turning within and talking to God more, and working on becoming more Spiritual. I asked God to let it be the time for me to develop my Mediumship, and be able to communicate with Spirit. I also asked my guides to help me to obtain that wish.

One day at work, I walked up to the front of the store, and a cashier whose name was Agitha, called me over to her. She handed me her ring and asked me to read it. I told her I had tried Psychometry before without any results, but she asked me to try anyway. I am glad she was persistent. I didn't think I would get any impressions from her ring, but to my surprise, when I shut my eyes, I saw a gold ring. I asked her if someone was going to give her a ring?
She said, "Who would give me a ring?"
I said "I don't know, but I see a beautiful gold ring for you."

A few days later, she walked up to me and excitedly held out her hand and showed me a pretty gold ring. When I asked her where she got it, she said her sister from Texas had just sent it to her. She was very amazed at my accuracy and told several associates about my newly acquired gift. Later that day, I went back to the receiving area. Candi, the manager back there, said Agitha had told her about my ability and she asked me to read her watch. When I did, I saw a dark haired woman as what appeared to be an angel looking down over her. When I described what she looked like, Candi said it was probably her mother who had passed over, because it fit her description. It was a beautiful sight to behold, and it made me feel very safe. It didn't sink in at first, as to what was happening. I didn't realize my prayers were being answered until the young woman named Dora, who worked along side Candi, asked me to read her ring. When I held her ring and closed my eyes, I saw the cutest little beige dog, and he was sitting and starring at me as though he was just waiting.

I asked Dora, "Do you have a beige dog?"

She said, "Yes, I have two, and they are brown and beige."

I said, "No, just beige," and described it more in detail.

She said, "Oh! Judy, that is my dog that hung himself on his chain, when I was eight years old, and I had always wondered if he was all right."

I looked at her, and she at me, with tears in our eyes, and we both knew that our wishes had been granted. She knew that her dog was all right, and I was able to communicate with Spirit. I didn't have any idea what it would be like to see Spirit, but that day when I left work, I was on a Spiritual high, that I felt I would never come down from. I knew then that I had the faith and courage to do what I wanted to do with my life.

After the other employees found out that I had this gift, I had plenty of practice with Psychometry. So much so, that I couldn't even take a break without someone wanting me to give them messages. It got so bad that I had to say, no more because they were draining my energy, and I needed that for my job. Every time, Pam and Jan were certain we wouldn't get busted doing readings, they invited me up to the office to practice on them. It was really exciting, to be able to see the visions that gave them so much important information for their lives.

One day, some of us employees were in the break room, and one of the other department managers named Patsy, asked me to read her ring. I had previously given her a message about her cat that was in Spirit. I closed my eyes with her ring in my hand, and I saw her in a meadow getting passionate with a young man. As I relayed the information, she looked at me with surprise and embarrassment and she never asked for a message again.

Another person that always seemed glad to have me give her information, was Dorothy. She was a divorcee, and would always ask my advice about one thing or another. When I first started giving her advice, she was interested in a man, named Layman, who also worked for the company, but he didn't seem to return her feelings. I told her that he would in time, and that they would end up getting married and stay married until death. While reading her Mother's ring, I was able to see that she was going to have huge problems with her teenage daughter, Sammi, but she would grow out of it. Sammi started giving her a lot of trouble shortly after that. She was sneaking out to meet boys, and a lot of other things that a young girl shouldn't be doing. It really caused Dorothy a lot of worry, just as I said, but as her daughter got a little older, she tamed down. I also saw a lot of problems for her son, Terry, but he would also turn his life around and get his act together, and he did as he got older. I gave Dorothy a lot of information that she said was very helpful to her in sorting out things that she had to deal with. Dorothy and Layman got married in time, and stayed married, until his death of complications from surgery.

The person that I got plenty of practice with was Beth, a young lady that worked in my department. She was forever more asking me to give her a reading. It was very exciting to sneak back into the stockroom and lay out the cards for her. It was also nerve racking, with the fear of being caught doing readings instead of our work. As I look back, I wonder how I was able to tune in so well, since I was not able to relax enough to totally concentrate on the cards. Thank God, none of the bosses found out that my stock room was also a place where I was practicing doing readings. Since Beth and I worked side by side, I would do a mini reading for her almost daily. I got to know her better than anyone in her life. She would always seem excited to get to work to see me. She said that I had all the answers to help give her a new out look on any situation, just by looking at my magic cards. She called me her Guru, and said that I was always there when she needed me. I feel I did what I did for her, because I cared about her, as she did me. She was always there to help me in some way. I bought her a deck of Tarot cards like mine for her birthday, and tried to share some of my knowledge on the subject with her. She worked with them some, but didn't pursue them as I did. To this day, of all the readings that I did for her over the years, she still reminds me of the day we sneaked into the stockroom at work, and I laid out the cards for her. I saw someone that she didn't know very well, would call her "from out of the blue," about a blond haired, blue eyed male. He drove a white car, while traveling a lot of hours for work. She said that even with all the details I had given her, she thought, "Yeah right." Nevertheless, just four days later, a high school friend's younger sister called her. Beth hadn't had any contact with her friend for about a year, so for her to hear from the friend's sister, was really "from out of the blue." The girl told Beth that she worked with a really nice guy, who was unattached because he had a hard time meeting girls because of his work. Beth's curiosity was getting the best of her, so she asked what the young man looked like. The young lady said he had blond hair and blue eyes. She wanted to know if it was okay to give him Beth's telephone number. Beth said it was fine. When the man called, he said his name was Rick, and he sounded nice so she agreed to meet him. Beth was totally shocked when he pulled up in a white car, that he used for traveling many hours a day as a salesman. They started dating, but it only lasted a few months because he was always busy working.

In other readings for her, I kept seeing a dark featured young man that she would be meeting through her sister. He would be well to do, and have a little black sports car. I felt they would get along quite nicely, and it would turn into a serious relationship that would end in marriage. Every time I would read for her, he would be in the cards. I kept saying it was getting closer, and she would say, "Yeah right," because a lot of time had passed and she had not met him. Each time, in response to her remark, I would tell her to wait and see, because I knew it would happen. I suppose, she thought it would happen in four days, like the last guy that I told her about. I kept reminding her that I was not always good with timing.

My retail job continued to go as usual, too much work in doing a job that I no longer enjoyed. I was having back pain from an injury, that I had sustained at work, so it was hard trying to do my job as I had done before. One night, I dreamed I went in to work the next day, and the store manager had moved some pillow racks and tables from the way that I had them displayed. When I went in to work the next day, the racks and tables had been moved and looked exactly as I had seen them in my dream. That was really a weird feeling when I saw it. I felt that could have been an out of body experience, rather than a dream. I remember telling another employee around that time that I felt they were going to get rid of the store manager near the seventh of May. It didn't come about until two years later but it was around the date that I had said. The manager got sent to another store as assistant manager. Note: You will probably notice that many times, I mentioned that something didn't happen until quite sometime later than I had foreseen. I have seen events coming six years in the future, and might think it will be much sooner. That's because there is no time in the Spirit World, so I'm not always good at timing events.

I felt I needed more practice, so I began to do a few readings at my apartment, for co-workers and friends. One of these associates, was a lady named Kathy. She also brought her sister with her. On a return visit, she told me that all the things that I had predicted for her sister previously had come to pass. I had read for them about three months prior. Her sister had her husband's retirement benefits taken away from her. I saw that it was due to a deceitful situation. I stressed the fact to her that it would be returned soon, and although she was pleased to hear that, she was certain it couldn't happen. She was just visiting here for a short time and was very unhappy with her life. I saw she would soon move to Florida, near her brother, and she would fare very well because of this. Kathy told me later, that her sister had indeed moved to Florida. She had also received the retirement benefits back and she was very happy at the time. That was very good news to hear, because she was in a very bad frame of mind when I had seen her. It's always good to know that when things seem at their worst, God knows what needs to be done. I saw a move for Kathy, at a distance, and I felt this move was going to reunite her with an old love. At the time of the reading it didn't mean anything to her, but she came back about a year later for a last reading, before she left town. Since I had seen her, she had been down to Tennessee, and had run into her ex-husband that she had been briefly married to when she was very young. They realized that they still cared for each other, after almost fifty years and decided to pursue a relationship again. He asked her to move down south so they could get to know each other again, and she did. That made me think that some things are meant to be, even if it does time.

As time went on, I continued to practice Psychometry more, and I seemed to be getting better at it. I had gone out one night after work to our usual hangout. I talked to some people that I knew, including John, a cop friend of mine who was there. John and I had been talking for awhile when I decided to leave. When I started to go, he offered to walk me to my car. On the way out, I noticed a ring on his hand, and ask if I could see it. When he gave me the ring, I closed my eyes, and something struck me as being funny, so I started laughing. I said, "I don't know what it means, but I see a car parked close to a corn field, and I think it is very funny." He laughed, and said that one night when he was out patrolling, he saw a car parked near a corn field. When he got out to investigate, he found a woman going to the bathroom in the corn, and it turned out to be a somewhat embarrassing situation. I could also see a dark colored car coming toward me head on, with the silver grille very clear and I felt very afraid. I ran into John the next day and he said when he left there that night, he was driving down the road and there came a black car with a silver grille toward him in his lane. He was lucky to miss a head on collision by swerving off the road. He said he was now a believer.

Chapter 8

I was getting more intuned as the days rolled by. I got more practice and learned a lot from reading Tarot cards for myself. I would remember certain things that I picked up from the cards, and then compare them to things that happened. I would then tell myself, "Now I know what that card meant." I think that working with the cards in that way, helped me to add some of my own meanings to them. Studying books on different subjects and using some of the things I learned to put with my own thoughts and feelings, were also very helpful with my development.

In that way, my work would be more a part of me than that of a teacher. In this line of work, I think that you need to put yourself into it, if you are going to be successful at it. Any knowledge that I have acquired about my work, has been self taught from studying on my own, except the basic astrology that I learned from Geri. So it doesn't always mean that you have to take classes to be able to learn the things that hold your interest.

After reading for my friends for quite sometime and gaining a little more confidence in myself, I had the opportunity to make my first public appearance as a Psychic, through Geri. Jill, who had sent me to see Geri previously, had asked her to do a metaphysical program for an organization that her husband worked for.

It was such a big event, that Geri asked myself and two other Readers to participate with her. Needless to say, I was doubtful that I was yet good enough to read out in the public. Geri assured me that I was, and that she needed my help, so I agreed to give it a try. I'm very glad that I did, because Jill, who was in charge of putting on the event, told me that I had been a big hit. So, January 1989, was a very important time in my life for my Psychic work. It made me feel very good that those people had accepted my work so well, and it made me realize I was finally ready to do readings for the public. It also gave me the encouragement to start advertising in the local newspaper and promoting my work in other ways.

People that came to see me would quite often send other people to me. Referrals became very important to me, and I think that is due to the fact, that I try to be Spiritual with my work. I also like to treat my clients like real people, who trust me enough to take my advice. I am very down to earth with my work, and I don't use a lot of fancy words that someone would not understand. I still have my Southern accent, even after being in the North all these years, but that's fine because I just want to be myself. When a client sits down with me, I like to make them feel comfortable, because a lot of people that come to see me are a little nervous. They expect to see a lady with a long dress, turban, and lots of fake jewelry. Not to mention, the dark room and crystal ball. Well, I do have a crystal ball, but it is not spooky. Nevertheless, when I open the door, they see an average looking lady with jeans, sweater, sneakers, and a smile on my face. They say, "You're not what we expected to see." My reply is, "Good" because that means I'm my own person."

I want people to enjoy their reading as much as I enjoy my work. I try to be as positive with my readings as I can, but sometimes that isn't always possible. Even when I see negative situations, I always try to impress upon my clients, that even negative things have a positive side. One of my favorite phrases that I used for many of my clients was, (negative thoughts bring negative things, and positive thoughts bring positive things.)

I also try to bring humor into the reading when I can, but not so much that they can't still take the reading as very serious work.

I never want to be known as a gloom and doom Psychic, but to be known as a lady that loves her work and knows what she's doing. Also known as someone able to help people to cope with some of their problems that they have to deal with in their daily lives.

Yet the main reason, I would like to be known is that I am a lady who is able to give them hope, no matter how bad their situation may be. As long as there is hope, things will surely improve. I try to convey to my clients, that a positive attitude is very helpful, and talking to God can bring remarkable results.

It makes me feel very good inside when one of my clients comes back and tells me that I had helped them to be able to get through a bad situation. As long as I get this kind of feedback, I know I am doing the kind of job that I want to do. If I can send people away with a smile on their face, and the hope to get through another day or another month, I have done the best that I can do.

I moved right along with my life that summer, feeling more self assured than I ever had, because God seemed to be blessing me in many ways. My clientele was growing larger and I was really enjoying my work. I was getting a lot of positive feedback that I was very accurate with my information I was giving my clients.

It made me feel very good inside, to be able to give them some sort of guidance. Yet the feelings inside were not that of ego, but of inner peace.

(I never forgot for a minute, that someone up there gave me all the information that I needed, and I felt very honored that they chose to help me.)

Chapter 9

As time went on, I began to realize that I needed to study more about becoming a Medium. I had wasted enough time, and I felt it was time to go for it.

(A Medium, is someone who is able to communicate with the Spirit World). There are two kinds of Medium, trance and mental. A trance Medium is someone that goes into deep trance, is not in control, and allows a Spirit to come in and use their body and voice to communicate with the living. A mental Medium stays fully aware of their surroundings and in control, while delivering information that they receive from a Spirit.

(My desire was to be a mental Medium, and be fully aware of what was going on around me when I channeled Spirit.)

I recall, telling some of my regular clients that was what I wanted to learn to do. They informed me that they thought I already did, because I had a different personality when I was doing a reading, than when I was just talking to them. I started to notice that, after they brought it to my attention, and had to agree. When I am working, I am much more in charge and very out going, happier, and sometimes even funny. I would say, my sense of humor is very pronounced then. However, when I am not working, I am a much more serious person.

That's when I communicated to my higher Spirit Guide that I wanted to become a good Medium, and began to realize that they had already been helping me. With my willingness to learn, my guides have been very helpful, and seemed to be working overtime to help me with my development. Although I have many guides, my main guide is named Tawl Horse, and he was a young Indian Medicine man. His father and grandfather were also Medicine men, before leaving the physical world. Tawl Horse helps me with readings, and also with healings.

(A guide is an entity from the Spirit World, who gives someone on the Earth plane help and direction with their lives.)

I felt that other than reading books on this subject, and practicing, the next best place to learn more about channeling, would be at a Spiritualist church. I had met a young woman through Geri, and her name was Carla. We had become better acquainted while doing some Psychic events around the area. She went to the First Spiritualist church here in town, and invited me to go there with her. It was strange, that as many different religions I had tried in my life, I don't ever remember feeling as comfortable as I did there. I had been to many churches, from Baptist to Catholic, and was baptized Lutheran, but I knew when I left the little church, that was how I wanted to feel about God, and my life. The only basic difference in that religion and what I had been brought up to believe, was that it believed that anyone could communicate with the Spirit World. I learned quite a bit about the Spiritualist religion, and I was in agreement with it. I even learned that Abraham Lincoln was a Spiritualist, and that was very surprising to me. That was the beginning of me becoming a Spiritualist, and a member of that little church. I was really happy with my religious beliefs for the first time in my life. Reverend Tingley, who was the pastor of the church, had a lot to do with that. He also had a lot to do with encouraging me to develop my Mediumship further. I had been going to the church for awhile, when my niece Teri, asked me one Sunday if she could go along. I told her, of course she was welcome, since she is also interested in the Psychic Realm and the Spiritual side of it. Reverend Tingley was giving Spirit messages after the regular service, and he came to us and asked if we knew a man named Red. He said he was there with love, and that he had a humorous personality. Teri and I looked at each other and said, "How did he know that?"

Red was my sister Ruthie's husband, whose real name was James, and he had just passed over and was buried two days before. Red was a very funny man, and had much love for all of the family. It was a wonderful experience to receive the message from him.

The church put on Psychic events from time to time, for fund raisers. I was one of the Psychics that read at their events, and I developed a good following from that. So between the event for the church, and another Psychic event that I read for, I was becoming pretty well known in town. Of course, my referrals added to that fact. I learned that word of mouth is your best form of promoting your work. I always tried to do a good enough job for my clients, so they will feel comfortable enough with me to send other people to see me. That policy has turned out to be very good for me.

Chapter 10

Through the church, I met many interesting people. We talked about the subjects that I was already interested in and had been learning. I still was putting more effort into my Tarot cards, but I knew it was time to expand my horizons.

Since I had been told I had a healing hand, I started working more on studying about healing, and finally felt I knew enough about it to give it a try. (A healing is laying your hands on a person's shoulders, or the problem area, and saying a prayer as you send healing energy into that person.)

My first attempt at doing a healing was for my daughter. She gets a sore back often, from tension and bending her head down while studying or reading. I put all of my learning and energy into that healing, but there was no results. I thought it would really be great, to relieve pain for the person that I cared most for. Even though I tried a few times, it didn't work, so I thought it's not time for me to do that either. I felt that maybe God wasn't ready to use me as a channel for healing yet. So I put that aside also, as I had done with my first try at Psychometry, not realizing, that for some reason my healings didn't work very well for my daughter.

I also had a hard time trying to do a Tarot reading for her. I thought it was because I am so close to her, but that doesn't really explain it clearly because I read better for myself than any other reader can read for me. So being too close to the situation doesn't really seem to be the answer.

There is one thing that I found out I could do for her, and that was reading a candle flame. She was lying in bed one evening, and the only light in her room, was a candle that was on the headboard of her bed. I went in and sat on the side of her bed, and we were talking. As we talked, I began looking at the candle flame, and started to do a reading for her. I saw a young man, and described him, and told her how he would effect her life. I saw some events with her career, and how some things would transpire. It was really strange, how the flame would change into different shapes that I was able to read. It seemed so easy to do and I wasn't even trying, because I didn't even know I could read it before I sat down and began looking at it.

I was starting to get a little frustrated with myself, and wondering if Tarot cards were going to be my main tool for using my ability, since that was what seemed to come easiest. I started to read more on meditating, and I found that there are many ways to meditate. Some books I have read, tell people they need to meditate for long periods of time, but I never found that to be true for me. My meditation time is a few minutes before I fall asleep at night, also the relaxed time that I have as I wake up in the morning. I have found that the best time, I can meditate is when I'm getting dressed and putting on my makeup. I really don't know why that is such a special time, unless it's because I am concentrating entirely on myself, and that is my own time for me. As I do that, I let my mind wander, and I have received some very important information from Spirit.

So, I feel that each person has to find their own way of meditation, and there is no set way to do it. I also think it is just taking a little time for you to tune in and listen to yourself. It doesn't always take a long time and a quiet dark room. Each individual will meditate the way are comfortable with.

Chapter 11

It was at that time in my studies, that I had another experience with my associate Beth, this time involving healing. As we were working together one day, we were chatting, and I was giving her more details about my Psychic studies. She found it very interesting when I was talking about how I wished to develop in different areas, and that I had been working harder at it. I started telling her about trying to do the healing for Vicki, but didn't have any results. She said she was having a problem with a sore heel on one of her feet. She had just been to New York, and from all the walking that she did, her shoe had rubbed her heel and it had gotten inflamed. She asked me to give her a healing, and I said that it probably wouldn't work, because I hadn't had any success with it before. I looked at her heel and it was so red, you could almost feel the pain by just looking at it. I put my hand on her heel and said a prayer of healing, and told her it should feel better soon. The next morning, Beth came in to work and said the pain was worse. I apologized that it didn't help, and said I had tried my best to make it work. A few hours later she went to lunch, and when she got back, she couldn't explain what happened, but suddenly the pain disappeared. We checked her heel, and the redness had also disappeared. I realized then, that it was time to start using this gift more, because it seemed as though it had finally started working for me. After the healing incident with Beth, I have helped many people.

Through God's guidance and healing energy, there were healings for many other more serious things. My sister June, became one of the people who most definitely believed in my healing gift. One day, I went over to her house, and she was complaining that her arm was sore from working. She said that it hurt so badly when she let it hang down, it felt like her hand would fall off, and she couldn't raise her arm very far. She asked for a healing, and I gave her one. The next day, when I saw her and asked how her arm was, she replied that it was fine except one little spot by her elbow. I gave her another healing. The next day, she said the pain was gone and she could raise her arm over her head, once again. On another occasion, she hurt her foot at work. She had gone to the doctor to have it checked, and he told her it looked like it could be serious because it was all inflamed. He even suspected a blood clot, and sent her for a CT scan. Between the doctor visits and the CT scan, she asked me for a healing, and I gave her one. That night, when she went to bed, she said her foot hurt her so badly that she would have welcomed the thought of having it cut off, just to relieve the pain. She suffered through the night, and when she got up in the morning, after walking on it for a few minutes, it seemed fine. She went and had the CT scan anyway, to be sure nothing was wrong. The doctor was so amazed that the test showed nothing, he was at a loss for words. He couldn't explain how it could be in such good shape so soon. Later, she said that her worker's compensation insurance was giving her a hard time about paying the medical bills because they had found nothing wrong. I guess, I should have waited until after the test to give her the healing. The healing episodes with Beth and June made me realize that sometimes with a healing the pain gets worse for a short time before it gets better, probably because it's working its way out. However, sometimes the pain just goes away; and sometimes the healing doesn't work at all. It is hard to understand why God only allows some, and not all people to be healed. As I look back, there were many more healings that worked, than didn't. One day, my daughter's friend Heather called me and asked for a healing. She had been having problems with muscle control for awhile, and the doctors had just diagnosed her with Multiple Sclerosis. The test the doctors had given her had left her in such bad shape, she could hardly get off the couch. While I was doing the healing, I could feel the energy go all down her body inch by inch, and I could feel a tingle like an electric current as it did. It was a very intense feeling, and she said she could feel the same thing that I felt. Later, she called to say she was feeling so much better, she was able to run the vacuum that same day; and she returned to work the next day. Some time had passed, and she called me again and said she was really sick, and asked for another healing. As I was giving it, the same feelings of energy and electricity happened. Again, it worked well for her, and she is still doing well. I found out from those experiences with her, that for some reason, healings by telephone seem to work very well. Maybe, because the current in the phone lines intensifies the energy that I send out.

It seemed as though I was getting to use my healing hand more and more as time passed. I had another interesting session with a client, whose name is Sarah. When she got here, she said she knew when she saw my ad in the paper that I was the person she was supposed to see. She had called some other ads and did not feel right with them. She was a young lady of nineteen going on ninety, and seemed like a very old soul who was pretty well informed about metaphysical subjects. Although she knew about developing on the subject, no one had taught her how to control it and shut off what she wasn't comfortable with. I told her that she controlled what information she received. If she had a positive attitude, and was spiritual with her thoughts, then she would receive more positive information. I could feel that she had been around some negative forces that were confusing to her, and were taking a lot out of her physical well being. I offered her a healing that she gladly accepted. When I was done with the healing, she said she felt like a new person that had just had heavy burdens lifted from her. She left with a positive feeling that all was well.

I had another call one day, from a lady who said she needed to see me. She seemed very urgent, so I worked her into my afternoon schedule. She was a new client, and when she got to my home, she said she had seen my ad in the newspaper. Although, there were other Psychics listed, she knew I was the one she was supposed to see. I didn't question her about it, because I wasn't sure what it meant. I had her to sit down and talked with her briefly before the reading. She informed me that she was having problems with her eyes, and I offered her a healing. She accepted the offer. Her eyes were all red and swollen, and she seemed nervous. When I laid my hands on her shoulders and started giving the healing, there was an awful feeling of chills and other weird feelings going up my arms, but I continued the healing. When I was finished, I sat down. I proceeded to tell her that I had given lots of healings before, but I had never had bad feelings like that, and I did not like those feelings. She said the reason I had those feelings was because a witch had put a hex on her and it had affected her eyes. I didn't know what to think. Even though, I knew that witchcraft was all around, I hadn't ever dealt with it before. It took me quite a few minutes to shake off the negative feelings. As I was doing the reading, I could see her eyes starting to look better. By the end of the reading, she looked like a different person. She felt much better, and thanked me for helping. The next day when I went to work, I mentioned the experience to a young man that came in to put bicycles together for my department. He had told me previously that he was into Wicca, so I thought he might help me to understand. I asked if he thought that I had done the right thing by giving the woman the healing, because I didn't know if it was her imagination or if it was real. He said that whether it was real or not, it was to her; and if I had the ability to help her, then I had done the right thing. She came back a short time later, with the same problem. Again, I gave her a healing. I then informed her that I couldn't keep draining my own energy if she wasn't going to help protect herself. I taught her how to use the white light of Christ for protection, and said to use it at all times. She wanted me to come to the place where she lived and say a prayer and send healing light in. I went to the place where she stayed, and she said the witches had put a spell on her hip, and she could hardly walk. I gave her another healing and said a prayer, for God to send in the white light to heal her and her home. I left, and I haven't heard from her since. I hope all is well with her. (I don't know much about Witchcraft, but I do know enough to know, that all witches are not evil and cast bad spells. Some are good spiritual people, and use their spells to better mankind, and for healing.) Their beliefs are different than mine, but as long as they don't harm anyone, I think they have a right to believe however they wish. I feel that way about any religion. I am very opened minded about people having the right to believe however they want. The only time I would find fault with anyone's religion, would be if they try to use it to harm someone, or force their opinion on someone else. I don't have much patience for any religion that thinks their way of believing is the only way, because in my opinion, only God knows what is the right way. There are many names for the higher power that I call God. Whatever anyone calls him, having faith will bring the same end result for all of us.

As I used my healing hand more, I realized that not only was my Medicine Man Guide helping me with the healings, but he was also very helpful while I was doing readings. He would help me make accurate predictions when a client had health problems that needed to be checked out by a doctor.

One of these clients, was a young woman named Venessa. Every time, I would read for her, I kept picking up that she had female related health problems. I felt she might need surgery to correct the problem. After much encouragement from me, she went to the Doctor, and found out she needed a hysterectomy. After that was done, she came back to see me and said that she was having problems with her recovery. I told her that I still saw more female problems and more surgery because they had missed something, and if need be, to get a second opinion. She stopped by where I worked a short time after that, and said "Thank God," she had listened and gotten another opinion. The doctor had found cysts in her breast and a large cyst on an ovary that they had left. They had to do more surgery to remove them. She thought I had saved her life by being so persistent about her getting medical attention. She was grateful that she had paid attention to what I told her, and followed up on it.

Another situation, which was a little like that, was a woman named Lana. She had been coming to see me on a regular basis for quite sometime. Every time, I would read for her, I would also see female problems for her, and was even able to tell her where the painful area was located. She had been checked by a Doctor and was told it was stress related. Each time I saw her, I got a little more persistent, and felt that something needed attention and possibly surgery. I even got so insistent, that I suggested that she see my Gynecologist, which she did and he also told her it was stress. Well, I still wasn't satisfied and asked her to please get another opinion and ask for more tests. She finally found a Doctor who got down to the nitty-gritty and found out that she had endrometerosis. He did surgery and it turned out well. Happy outcomes like these makes you feel that you have a purpose in life. If in some way, you might have had a small part in helping someone be able to get the right help to save their life. There have been many other situations like the ones I mentioned, that I feel honored to have been of some sort of help, but for some reason these stick out in my mind.

Note: I don't in any way claim to be a doctor, or try to replace one, but I am sometimes able to foresee problems that need medical attention. In that case, I suggest to my clients that they seek medical attention and I am always willing to offer a healing along with their medical help. I have sometimes thought that some of my clients needed more than a psychic reading; instead they seem to need psychological counseling, and I suggested that they get the help that I was not trained to give them. As with the psychical problems, I offered a healing to go along with their professional help.

Chapter 12

I seemed to be getting more intuned and involved with my work as time passed. It was July 1989. Beth and I went out one night after work to one of my favorite night clubs. On our way inside, we passed by a red Firebird in the parking lot, and I said to Beth, "I am going to meet the person tonight that owns that car."
We went in, and though the place was crowded, it was boring, maybe because I had just gotten out of a relationship and didn't really want to be there. I had just told Beth that night that I was going to take a break from dating. Anyway, I really thought I was.

That was the night, I met my now husband, Bob. I noticed that a man kept staring at me when I passed by him. So, when Beth and I started to leave, I had to pass by him again. As I did, I said to him, "If you are going to keep staring, the least you can do is say hello." Of course, he did, and we talked briefly. He offered me a drink and I accepted a glass of water. We danced a couple dances and I told him Beth and I were leaving, since that was what we were in the process of doing before. He asked for my phone number and I gave it to him, thinking that I would play the game. I never expected him to call, and really didn't care if he didn't. I didn't think our encounter would turn into anything, as I left to go home. The next day he called me, and I asked him what kind of car he drove. He said, "A red Firebird,"
I said, "'No way."
I also found out that he is a Leo, a sign that I vowed I

would stay away from. That's what my ex-husband was, and I didn't want anything more to do with a Leo man.

Still, in spite of my fears, we began dating and he dragged me in hook, line, and sinker. It makes me wonder why we seem to go back into like situations that were mistakes in the past. It must be karma.

Sometimes, it takes us a long time to learn the lessons that we need to learn in this life. I am still trying to find out the things I am supposed to learn from my relationship with Bob. As time goes by, I am learning some things from him that I think I was supposed to learn from my ex. He reminds me so much of my ex-husband that it's unreal. Their temperament is a lot alike and most of their taste in food is similar. I mean, what are the chances of having two husbands that eat a lemon like it is an orange. They are the only two people that I have ever known that does that. The first time I saw Bob eat the lemon, I told him the past had come back to haunt me. I have had many Psychic dreams about both of them and the events came about just as I saw in my dreams.

Chapter 13

Not long after I met Bob, I started to make a lot of changes with my life, such as, selling my mobile home and moving into an apartment.

My brother in-law, whom we called Curly, helped me move. He was my sister Linda's husband, and Cindi's father. He put up blinds and curtains and also lent a hand with the other things that I needed a man's help with to get settled in the apartment.

Linda and Curly were the caretakers in our family. Cindi, who is an only child, was very close to her Mom and Dad, but she had an especially close bond with her dad. Anytime we needed anything done or any help, they were always there for the rest of our family.

Shortly after I moved into the apartment, I had a strange thing happen. I had a throw rug lying on the floor between my dining room and living room. It seemed to always move by itself, even though, it had a rubber backing on it and it was on carpet. Several times a day, I would have to move the rug, because it kept moving close to the table and chairs. After a few days of that, I said to myself, " Why is it doing that?"

At that moment, my sister Marg, whom had passed over earlier, came to mind. One of the things I remember about her when she was living was that she used to go around straightening their throw rugs all the time, like it was an obsession with her. It was baffling me, trying to figure out if it was really her, or my imagination. I woke up one morning around 4:00 a.m., and my eyes were drawn to look into the hallway.

I could easily see from my bed about fourteen feet away, a white shadow of a woman looking toward my bathroom and I just knew that it was Marg. I wasn't afraid, and felt very calm as I laid back down to go to sleep. When I woke up in the morning, the white figure was the first thing that came to mind. I tried to figure out if I had been awake or dreaming. I truly believe I was awake. That night, I dreamed that I went into my kitchen, and looked up toward the ceiling and saw pretty lights. I asked, "Was that you Marg, with the rug and in the hallway?" I heard her voice say, "Yes." Up until that time, since I had been in the apartment, I sensed that someone was there and it made me a little nervous. I kept having a feeling that someone was in the room with me and I would look around to see who it was. After the sighting and the dream those feelings left; I felt comfortable, and the rugs stopped moving.

Exactly four months after Curly helped me move into the apartment, he unexpectedly died of a heart attack. It was the day after Christmas, and I had just gotten home from work. The phone rang, and it was my sister Betty, telling me that Curly was dead. I couldn't believe what I was hearing. We had just seen him on Christmas Eve. He had shown me a bathroom that he had just remodeled, and was feeling very proud of his job well done. He was only forty-eight years old, but he had always said that he wouldn't live to be forty-nine. This had to be the biggest shock the family had ever had. Although, there had been several other deaths in the family, his death had been so sudden and unexpected. I went with Linda up to the hospital where they had taken him, and I went into the room with her to say good-bye. I could see him lying there on the table dead, but I could hear his laughter fill the room with happiness. Later that night, his daughter Cindi was at my place. She had her father's wedding ring, and asked me to hold it in my hand and see if I could pick up any information from it. I closed my eyes and said, I see his grave next to a tree with snow on it. That didn't make sense because there was no snow. Yet, when they went to the cemetery to arrange for his grave, it was beside a tree and it had snow on it.

I went with them to pick out the casket. Cindi was walking along side me and for some reason, we walked right up to a particular casket, as though we had been guided there. I said to her, that it looked like something her father would pick out and she agreed.

Another sister of ours, Ruthie, and her daughter Jackie went there with us. They called Linda, Cindi, and I, over to look at another casket. When I walked over to see the one they were looking at, I had an awful feeling of dread. They asked what I thought of it, and I blurted out that Curly wanted the one Cindi and I had been looking at. It was strange, that as soon as we walked back over to that one, the feeling of dread left, and I told them so. Cindi seemed to feel it also. Linda got the one he wanted. It was very nice, and Curly made a good choice.

Just five months before, God had sent Cindi a baby boy named Devon, and Curly was quite the happy grandfather. I guess, God knew exactly what he was doing, because that baby was the only thing that helped Linda and Cindi cope with their loss.

It was hard for the whole family to adjust to losing Curly. That sad situation, along with other things, have helped me to learn over the years that when I am in emotional turmoil, my Psychic ability becomes stronger. It seems to make me a stronger person, and it also makes it easier for me to take charge and be more in control of my life.

Chapter 14

I started being more active in the church at the time of Curly's death. I felt I had grown a lot in the past few years because I was comfortable enough to get up in church and give messages from Spirit, when asked. I was also honored to be asked to do healings at the healing chair.
(Serving at the healing chair, is a part of the service where a healer lays their hands on a person's shoulders, and through prayer sends them healing energy).
Since I began doing that my Mediumship has gotten stronger every day. Being able to get up on the platform and give messages from the Spirit World was a new experience for me, and it was very exciting. It was gratifying to be able to give someone that I didn't know, a message from a loved one. It felt great when I could give them a name they understood and news to go with it. They seemed to find much comfort from it.

For some reason, for about two months, I had been asking my sister Linda to go to church with me. I usually don't keep asking anyone to go, but I kept trying and she agreed to go the following Sunday.

That Sunday, when I was getting ready to go to church, I realized why it was so important for her to go. Curly came through to me and said he was going to bring us a message. I had been waiting for a long time to see if I would receive a message from him in church. I guess, he felt it was important for Linda to be present when he did. Just like he said he would, he gave her a message through the Pastor. It was really exciting when she was getting the message, because I could feel Curly's presence behind us. What was funny, was he had a hard time getting his name through.

(Which is common, because sometimes, it's hard to understand what someone in Spirit is saying.)

The pastor asked her, "Who is Russell, no, Rush, no, Ru?"

I told him, he should give up because he would never pick up such an unusual name.

Then I asked, "Are you trying to say Rufus?"

He said, "Yes, Rufus."

That was, Curly's birth name. I asked the pastor to try and pick up his nickname, and give it to me, when he saw me again. The next time I was at church, Reverend Tingley and I were talking about the speech I would be giving in the near future. He ask me if I knew someone named Charlie.

I said "No."

"Carly."

Then I realized who it was.

I said, "How about Curly?"

He said, "Yeah, Curly."

I told him, that was Linda's, husband's nickname, that I had asked for. Curly has come through several times since then, and one of the ways he lets us know it is him, is that he tells the pastor he died fast of a heart attack.

I have been giving more messages in church as time goes by. It is really strange when the information comes, I sometimes hesitate to repeat it, for fear of being wrong. Then, when I tell the person whom it is meant for, they usually understand the message. One of the messages was for an older man that was in church with his wife. A middle aged man came through in Spirit, and wanted me to relay to his brother that he was there. He said his name was Fred, and he showed me that he wore a dark blue uniform to work, where he worked very hard. He had much love for his brother; Fred wanted his brother to know that he was going to help him with his game, while showing me a small white ball that looked like a golf ball. When I asked the man if he played golf, his reply was "No." I told him, I didn't know what Fred meant when he said he would help with his game, but I thought the little white ball was a golf ball. The man's wife spoke up and said, "He probably meant he would help him with the lottery game, because he always plays, and it is a little white ball."

A Spirit message came through for a woman that was there. It was from a man who said he was her brother Jerry. The message was so clear that I couldn't believe it. He was a very funny person, and he was kidding about his red hair that he didn't like. His message was short but very uplifting because he had such a good sense of humor. When I was giving the lady her message, she had a big smile on her face and was very happy that her brother was there. She said, that when her brother was alive, he was a very funny man, and he didn't like his red hair. Another story comes to mind of Spirit messages. When I was on the platform at church once, a message came to me to give to three ladies who were seated together. I didn't know anything about these ladies. To one of them, I asked if she had seen a tornado or whirlwind, or was that how she was feeling? Behind the tornado, I saw a beautiful pink sky. That was about how she was feeling because she had lost her aunt, and they called her Pinkie.

To one of the other ladies, Pinkie was showing me a Christmas tree for her. The lady said that Christmas is her birthday, and Pinkie was her sister. Pinkie told me to tell her sister to sort through the stacks of papers and look for twenty near the bottom of the pile. She also wanted them to know that they would have a very good Christmas season. The lady came up to me after church, and laughingly said, "You think you are smart don't you?"

When I asked her why, she said her father had just passed over and her mother had brought her some papers to sort through. She had missed the one pile that had an insurance policy for twenty thousand dollars. I told her not to stop looking because there was a separate pile and I saw the number ten. She said that would really help her mother because she didn't even know about the policies. The next Sunday, she came up to me after church, and said I was right about the policies. The ladies were very happy about that. I really feel blessed when I can give people information that can help them with their lives.

I decided to try another Spiritualist church, here in town. It was smaller than the church I had been going to, but I felt very comfortable there. There seemed to be some very caring and gifted people there. Linda went with me. I enjoyed it so much, I continue to go there from time to time.

We received some positive messages when we were there. I was able to give messages that I had received during the message service to a couple of people after church. I was glad Spirit was there to help while I was visiting a new Church.

Chapter 15

On a previous, but rare occasion, I did a reading for Linda, before her grandson was born. I told her, I saw a baby in her family, soon. We found out later, that Cindi was pregnant at that time with Devon, and no one knew about it. Since then, I have done other readings for Linda, to give her advice about her job situation and general information.

One time, Curly came through and gave me a message to give to Linda. It was about an insurance policy from a company that he used to work for before he died. It was in a gray box, and he gave me the number twenty. I don't think Linda ever really looked for the policy, because she didn't believe it. She doesn't know how helpful I have been with bringing other people messages about lost policies. Maybe, one day she will decide to look for it. I have no doubt that it is there waiting for her.

I recall one time, when she was having some problems with her car. It was leaking fluid, and a mechanic told her there was something wrong with the engine and wasn't worth getting it fixed. I told her he was wrong, he was just trying to cheat her out of her car, because it was just an old hose that wasn't connected well. I kept bugging her to have someone else check it. She admitted that he said she should junk the car, but when she said she wouldn't, he told her if she wanted to sell it cheap, he knew someone that needed a car. How amazing, that it went from being a junker, to a car that one of his friends could use. She had her neighbor check the car, and put a new hose on it at the spot where I told her it was not connected, and it worked. Shortly after that, it was leaking again and I told her something wasn't making a good connection. It was the radiator plug, because the neighbor didn't connect it good when he drained the radiator. Since she got that replaced, she hasn't had any more problems. There wasn't anything wrong with the motor, it was just a deceitful mechanic.

Since I am talking about car problems, I should mention Vicki and her car. It kept stalling out on her and we had taken it to several garages, but no one could find the problem. Every time, they would do something different and charge more money, but the problem still remained. One day, I took it to my husband's mechanic and I told him that I saw something that looked like an oil filter but it was smaller. I told him where it was located on the car, and he said it sounded like I was describing the gas filter. He replaced it and the car worked fine after that. Another time, she had a similar situation, but a different part, and I told them what the problem was. When they fixed it, I was correct. I have been able to give other people information about problems with cars. I guess, I must have a Spirit guide that was a mechanic, and I appreciate all the help.

It was at later time that I was able to give another family member some Psychic advice. June asked me to do a reading for her, which was very surprising, because she had never asked for one before. In fact, none of my family has taken advantage of my ability. Maybe, because they don't want me to feel because I am family that I am obligated to do readings for them. When June called for a reading, I assumed that something must be bothering her, since this was her first time asking me. I told her, I would tape a reading and give it to her when I saw her again. I did the reading and it was very disturbing, because I could see that her husband was cheating on her. There was so much deceit in the cards that they seemed to leap up off the table at me. The reading had so much negativity that I didn't tell June I had done it at first. I told Linda and Betty what I had seen, and that I was uncomfortable telling her about it. They didn't think I should tell her either, and I didn't until a week later, when June called me again and asked if I would do a reading. She thought something was going on with her husband, who had been working in the next state for many years of their marriage. I had thought over the years that he might be cheating on her. From time to time, I would ask her what he did with his money, because he made a good salary, but he was never a good provider for her. Every time, I would say anything, she would make up excuses for him that just didn't add up. I took the tape over to her the next day. We were going to the store, and I played it for her as we were driving in the car. Since I had taped the reading, she had started finding out some things about her husband, and most the things I had said on the tape had taken place in that short time. I saw a red-haired woman around him. It turned out that he had been living up there with a redhead for quite sometime, and that was where his money was going. Shortly after that, June filed for a divorce. I saw that he was going to deceive her. He delayed the divorce, and it took seven months instead of the usual three to be final. I also felt that he would lie and say that he was not working, so he wouldn't have to pay alimony, and he did. She still was awarded alimony, but I told her she would have a hard time getting it from him. Several thousand dollars have added up, and she still has not received any money. I wish, I had been able to give her good news about the situation, because she deserves something good. I am sure her goodness will pay off for her eventually, and God will send good things her way. As I remember my experiences with helping June, I have to mention her daughter Amy, and a strange thing that happened with her. I did a reading for her one evening, and I shut my eyes and saw a vision of her being in a field. Then I could see her as though she was in a cave with bars on the windows, and there was darkness all around. She felt very alone and afraid, but then I could see light coming through the bars. It seemed like she was in the dark and was looking to find a way out into the light. She was going up to her boyfriend Jason's house that night, and it was storming outside. I asked her not to go because there were fields by his house, and I was afraid something would happen to her. She went to Jason's house anyway, and nothing happened. She wasn't able to make sense of my vision until later. Shortly after that, Jason moved to Memphis, and he asked Amy to go with him. Because they were in love, she decided to go with him. She had never lived on her own that far from home before and she was very homesick. It got so bad for her that she decided to come back home. Of course, shortly after she came home, Jason came back home also. Amy found a good job as the office manager of a growing cleaning supply business, and she began going to college. Jason has become very responsible and they seem to get along just fine. So much so, that I predicted a marriage in the near future. Jason bought a little house, and Amy has been helping him with and remodeling. It is really pretty since they have been putting all the work into it.

She told me later, that the things I had described in my vision was exactly how she had felt when she was in Tennessee. She also said that her talks with me were very helpful and healing. Last year in the springtime, I did a reading for Amy and I told her that Jason was going to ask her to marry him in the fall around October. They were excited when they came to see me in September to announce their engagement, and their wedding that would be the following September.

They couldn't get the hall and Church for then, so they ended setting the date for October tenth. I guess in a round about way, I gave her the correct information, or at least she thought so. It does my heart good to know I was able to help my family in some way.

Since I am on the subject of my family, I guess now is a good time to talk more about them. I have done readings for my nephew Jeff, who is Ruthie's son, and he thinks I am a good Psychic. He came back later and let me know when things came about that I had predicted for him. He reminded me of the time I told him he was going to get some unearned money, and a dark featured man would have something to do with it. One day at work, his boss was going to buy lottery tickets and Jeff gave him some money and told him to play one for him. He won over three hundred dollars with the ticket, that his dark featured boss bought for him. He was very pleased when he told me about it. I have also read for Jackie, who is Jeff's sister, and her husband Chris. The first time I read for them, they had just met, and I told them they would be married. Jackie was insistent that she would never remarry, and I was just as insistent that she would. Chris told the girls at his office that I had predicted the wedding on our first meeting, also that he was a doctor. He was amazed that I came up with that information, since I didn't know him. I was surprised that he was a believer in my ability, because all people aren't. I taped a reading for Chris recently and Jackie said they had listened to it many times, and was amazed at its accuracy.

I have done a few readings for Teri, and her brother, Bruce. Teri is my niece that I previously mentioned, who went to church with me. They are my sister Virginia's offspring. Both Teri and Bruce say they have a lot of faith in my predictions. Teri reminds me from time to time, about the prediction that I made for her once, with information about the man that she would be having a relationship with in the future. It wasn't long after that, she met the man that I had described in great detail. They are now engaged to be married.

I have never done a reading for my sister Gertie, or my brother Jimmy, as they have never asked me to. I have only done one reading for my sister Betty. I think Gertie and Betty are a little afraid of my abilities. Jimmy is very Baptist, and I don't think he believes in my gift but his wife Rosemary does. I'm not sure whether their daughters Kim and Shelley do or not, because they live down South and I haven't really talked to them about me being Psychic. EC and his wife Lou definitely believed in my gift as you will see a little later. I read for one of their sons whose name is Roger, and he thought the reading was neat. I have never read for their other sons, Larry and Jim, or their daughter Becky, nor have I talked about my ability with them.

Whether Gertie realizes it or not, she uses Astrology when they plant their crops on their farm. One day, we were talking on the telephone and she was talking about planting something, and said she couldn't plant it while the moon was in the sign of the feet. (That is the sign of Pisces, because it rules the feet.) I'm sure she got that information from the Farmer's Almanac, rather than from an Astrology book.

I would like to tell about an incident that Betty told me about, with her ability to see Spirit. She and my other sister Marg, were close in age, and neither were ever married. They lived with Dad after Mom passed over, and looked after him, because he had a lot of health problems as he grew older.

After Dad died, Marg told Betty that she saw his Spirit in the kitchen of their house, and after Marg died a few years later, Betty saw her Spirit, also in their kitchen by the refrigerator. So, it appears there are other of my family members that were gifted with the ability to communicate with Spirit and I never realized it before.

Chapter 16

Another fall season came around, and our town brought in a new a professional hockey team. It is affiliated with the Red Wings, who is their mother team. Bob, Vicki, June, Beth, and I started going to all of the games. Although, Bob is an avid Red Wings fan and goes to all of their home games, I had only been to a few. I could take or leave hockey until the Toledo Storm came into being; we became loyal fans, and I learned to like hockey a lot.

There was a young man named Bruce, on the team, and he was my daughter's favorite player. The following Spring, I went through a lot of hassles to invite him to Vicki's surprise twenty first birthday party. Which because of him, turned out to be the best birthday party she had ever had. He brought along another Storm player named Greg.
I gave Greg a mini reading at the party, and as I closed my eyes, with my Psychic vision I saw an Indian chief. There wasn't a name or anything else with the message, so I wasn't sure what it meant. Greg told me that it probably meant his nickname was "Chief." I don't know if I gave him any helpful information or not, because there was so much noise that it wasn't a quality reading. I couldn't concentrate, therefore, I don't feel it did justice for myself or my Guides.

Of course, the girls had a great time. The guys turned out to be very pleasant young men, and because they had been so good to stop by, I offered them a complimentary Psychic reading, at their convenience.

The following hockey season started, and we

became better friends with Bruce. About a month later, he called to make an appointment for his free reading. He turned out to be one of the nicest young people that I have ever met. After I read for him, we were talking, and I was able to give him a message from his Guide, whose name is White Feather. That was a great experience for me, to be able to see his Guide and hear his name. When I told Bruce about White Feather, I wasn't sure if he would accept it, or think I was weird. I told him, he probably shouldn't say anything to the other team members, because they might think he was crazy. The next time I went to the game, I was surprised when I talked to Bruce and he told me that their trainer had drawn a white feather on the sleeve of his jersey. I couldn't believe that he had told the team, because most guys would be too macho to say anything. As we all know, everyone does not share these beliefs. That made me realize, that this young man was his own person. He even sent two of the other team mates for a reading, plus several other people that he knew, including his fiancée Shawna. When I was doing Tarot for Shawna, my clairvoyance went into focus, (Clairvoyance is being able to see visions or events with your third eye, your Psychic center, located between your eye brows.) and I described a man that she had known, who was dark featured and very good looking. I felt she was very close to him, and that he made her laugh a lot with his jokes. She knew immediately whom I was talking about. He was a man that came into where she worked, and he became a good friend. He always had a joke to tell, and he was always making her laugh while telling them. She said he had just died a month before, due to a motorcycle accident.

Bruce has been a true believer in my work. I gave him a bag of healing crystals, and he wore them when he played, even though, some of the guys did tease him about them. After I had given him the stones for

Christmas that year, he gave me a picture of himself on the ice. On the picture, he wrote a special message that said, "Judy, Thanks for the Psychic guidance, and Motherly concern." The picture is hanging on my office wall, along side my daughter and husband's pictures. In return for his picture, Vicki and I went shopping and bought him a plaque, with the picture of an Indian who looks like his Guide, White Feather. Bruce remained friends with my husband, daughter, and me. I would give him healings when he was injured, and I let him read some of my books on Psychic development and self healing. Many of the predictions that I made for him came about as I told him they would. I could really tune in to him at the games, and could tell before hand if he was going to score and how many goals he would get. I recall, telling him that almost two thirds through his third year here, he would get traded to a better position. The team did very well their first two seasons here. The first year they got as far as the play offs, and the following year they did even better. They won the Riley Cup. In one of Bruce's readings, I saw a move coming up in three weeks, and that it would be at Christmas time, because I saw a pine tree standing alone. I saw big ice, a lot of ice, maybe it meant a larger rink that he would be playing at. Then I saw a candy cane to my left, and I told him that it was going up, over, and down. I saw him taking some time off from playing. Just after that, they put him on the injury list for three weeks. After that, he went back to playing, but the coach was not giving him much ice time so he asked to be traded. He said he would be going to either Columbus or Raleigh. I felt better with Raleigh. That's where he ended up going. He and his fiancée moved on Christmas day. So that was the lone pine tree, and they couldn't even enjoy the holiday at home because they had a deadline to meet. I found out later, that their team name is the Ice Caps. I guess big ice doesn't get much bigger than Ice caps. The over, up, and down probably meant that Bruce was part of a three-way trade involving, Toledo, Ohio., Erie, Pennsylvania., and Raleigh, NC.

I talked to him after he moved and he liked it down there. He said he was getting more playing time and was playing better because it was a more relaxed environment, and he liked the coach. His team played here later and we were rooting for Bruce.

He and Shawna planned to move back here in the summer time to get married. Bruce didn't get to finish the season because he broke his hand and he decided then to give up hockey. They moved back here ahead of schedule.   I said he would play hockey again, but he insisted that he was done with the game.

Another hockey season ended, and our team won the Riley Cup again. That was two years in a row. I guess you can imagine whom they had to beat out in the final round, to win the cup. Yeah, Raleigh. That was amazing, since Columbus, ranked higher, going into the play-offs. I had told Bob before hand, that we would end up playing Raleigh for the win. It was a close situation, because Raleigh gave us a good fight. I predicted, that the coach, who helped them to be back to back winners, would not return the following season, and he didn't. Chief replaced him as coach.

We were invited to Bruce and Shawna's wedding and it was beautiful, just like the bride and groom. They are a lovely couple and deserve to be happy. I foresee a baby girl in the immediate future for them.

I must add, that I was right about Bruce playing again, because he has filled in several times, when our team was short of their regular players. He moved out West someplace, to work for a team, but he did not stay there long. He did not like the job, and came back here to put on a Storm uniform again. "He is far from being done with hockey."

Chapter 17

My friends, Geri and Mona, both moved down to Tennessee the same year at Christmas time, just as Bruce was moving to Raleigh. Mona and Geri now live within fifteen minutes of each other. They both have family down there. It sure was hard, having three of my good friends leave at the same time. I never had a chance to get lonely before, because I could pick up the phone and know Geri and Mona were only minutes away, but now they are hundreds of miles away. This was the first time in many years that I could say I was lonely. Oh, I have other friends, but they aren't the same as the ones that moved away. I suppose, that's another lesson that I need to learn, and I am sure that I will adjust in time.

Vicki and I went down to Tennessee to visit Mona and Geri, after they had been gone for awhile. She had vacation time and offered to go down with me. We spent time with them, and checked out the scenery. We went to the Smoky Mountains one afternoon. I had never been there before and it was absolutely beautiful. I really felt close to nature and to God. I wish I had more time to spend there. On the other side of the Mountains, was Cherokee, North Carolina; and we went to the Indian Reservation there. It was a good feeling, to be at the homeland of my ancestors.

Mona and Geri were very happy to have us visit with them, and tried to talk me into moving down there to be closer to them. I told them it was beautiful down there, but I didn't have any desire to live down there at that time.

Since I am talking about them, I want to tell about a couple of things that I predicted for them. When I first began reading cards for other people, I practiced some on Mona. The first time I read for her, I saw that she would be taking a trip over water with a romantic connection. She would fly there, and it would be a wonderful trip, most likely, a cruise. She said that I had to be mistaken, because she wasn't seeing anyone at the time, and furthermore, she knew she would never fly because she was terrified of flying. Well, it took about six years of me repeatedly telling her about her trip, before it happened. She met a man, and they fell in love. He won a cruise through work, and he invited her to go with him. Of course, they had to fly down to get on the ship, and she did that with great hesitation. They were gone for a week and she had a wonderful time. When she came back, she said it took long enough to happen, but it was just as I had said it would be.

In another reading that I did for Mona, I described in detail the new house that her daughter, Katie, was moving into in Omaha, including the park that was across the street from it. When she asked her daughter what her house looked like, she described it just as I had seen it in my vision. Mona was shocked that I had been able to see all of the details about it.

Geri asks me, from time to time, to do readings for her. Even though she is great at Astrology and she reads for herself, she said she likes the way I read Tarot cards. She thinks I can pick up more and be more descriptive about people and details, than she can with Astrology. I would like to tell about a prediction that I made for her about a surgery that she had. She asked me to do a reading for her, to see how her surgery would turn out. The surgery was to be the day before the full moon, and I told her I was nervous about her having it then. When I looked at the cards, they confirmed my feelings that there would be problems

70

with bleeding. I couldn't believe she was going to have surgery so close to a full moon, since with her knowledge about Astrology, she knew it was not a good idea to have it within five days before or after. "Especially before, as the moon is going toward its full phase."

(Some Astrologers say, if you have a choice, and it's not an emergency, you shouldn't plan surgery near the full moon, because the moon rules the tides and fluids, which could mean excessive bleeding.)

I asked Geri if she could change the date of her surgery, and she said she couldn't. She went ahead with it, and she had problems with bleeding. She had a hard time recovering because she got a blood clot as big as a golf ball on her incision that she had to keep having drained. Part of her surgery included sewing her bladder back into place, and afterwards, she had a lot of problems with incontinence. She had to have the surgery over again about three months later because it was not successful. I began sending her healings at that time, and she seemed to be getting better. She has had a lot of faith in my healings and me over the years.

Chapter 18

The following summer, I started receiving messages that I thought were my imagination. From time to time, I would hear someone say, "Ruthie is dying," but I would shake it off as my imagination, because as far as I knew her health was fine. I also would hear someone say, "EC is really sick," and I thought he was okay as well. Even with all the practice, it is still sometimes hard to understand that these messages are not just thoughts going through my mind. I feel, that maybe the reason is because I don't always want to hear that kind of information.

Shortly after that, in early fall, we found out that Ruthie had cancer. She thought she had it but she would not tell anyone, because there had been several deaths in my family due to cancer. She didn't want to put the family through any more worry. It was some sort of cancer that was in her lung and rib cage. Had it been caught in time, it would have been 95% curable, but in her case, it was too late. I gave her healings, but even though she said she wanted to get better, I don't believe that was completely true. One of her daughters, and her husband, had died in recent years, and I think she had given up so she could join them. Still, she put up a good front for us, and always tried to keep a smile on her face when we were around. We knew she was getting worse, and was in severe pain, so my niece and nephew decided to put her in a Hospice unit. They felt that she would do better there with constant medical attention. Around that time, I had a dream on a Wednesday night. I dreamed she died on Thursday and was buried on Monday, and I was having to ask for time off work. It turned out just like I dreamed, only it was two weeks later. She only lasted a couple of weeks there, and she seemed to have a peaceful transition. So maybe the healings that I gave her helped with that, if nothing else.

The day she died, I was getting ready for work, as I had to be there at 2:00. I was putting on my make up and doing my hair. I was kind of lost in my thoughts, when I heard a message go through my mind. My niece Donna, Ruthie's daughter who was in Spirit, said to me as clearly as if she was really there, "I am coming to get my Mom today."

I didn't know what to think. Like before, I thought it was my imagination. I went to work feeling low.

Usually, I can put a smile on my face, but I couldn't that day. I had only been at work about an hour when I got a call saying that the family was needed at the Hospice Unit, because my sister was ready to go anytime. I left immediately, and went up there. Just the day before, Ruthie had been alert and smiling, and now, she was in what appeared to be a coma. She had her eyes shut and was breathing hard. The only thing we could do, was sit and wait and pray that it would be an easy passing. I was sitting on a chair in the corner of the room. It was as though I could feel, and sort of see, her husband James' Spirit walk into the room and sit on the chair in the corner opposite me. It was around 7:00 p.m. then, and he said, "I am going to take her at 8:00 p.m." A little later, Ruthie's eyes opened and started rolling back. I looked at my watch and it was exactly 8:00. She kept hanging on, while breathing harder. While James' presence was sitting on the chair, their son in-law walked in and sat down on that chair. I laughed to myself, because Chris didn't realize he was sitting on his father in-law's lap. Around that time, I went to stand at the foot of Ruthie's bed, and thought it could be any minute that she would breathe her last breath. As I was standing there, it was as though my family members that were passed over, walked up to the foot of the bed to let me know they were there to help her go. My sister Virginia didn't seem to be with the rest of the family. I have not figured out why, but she never seemed to be around them.

Anyway, Ruthie kept hanging on, it seemed for some reason, she just couldn't let go. Then, Curly our caretaker, walked up closer to the foot of the bed and with his "take charge" attitude said, "I'll take her." Jackie had been trying to talk her mother through and let her know it was okay to go. It was only a few minutes after Curly took charge that my sister took her last peaceful breath.

Around the same time that we found out about Ruthie's illness, we also found out that my brother EC was very sick. It supposedly was an inflamed esophagus, and he had just had major surgery on his stomach. I think cancer might have been involved there, also. He was not recovering from the surgery very well, and I would give him a healing each time I would see him. It was as though, he had given up and wasn't trying. He would cry and say he wasn't going to pull through. He was so skinny and pale, I thought he could go at any time. I actually thought he would die before Ruthie. I went up to see him one day, and he was crying. He kept saying that he wasn't going to make it, and I started talking to him, or maybe, I should say, yelling. In other words, giving him heck, as I told him that Ruthie didn't have much hope, and she was still able to force a smile. He did have hope and wasn't taking advantage of it. No matter how many healings I gave him, it wouldn't help unless he started being more positive and believed that he would get well. He had to believe in the healings, and God would make him well. I guess the lecture worked, because within a day or so, he

74

was showing much improvement. He got out of the hospital and I continued the healings when I saw him. He seemed to be doing very well. He lived for about five years after that, although he had developed cancer. He had gone through all the treatments, and had gone into remission off and on. There were times that he would get so bad, that he would have to go back to the hospital, and the doctors would give up on him. I would go up and see him, and think that he would die any minute. Again, I'd give him a healing, and shortly after the healing, he would get color in his face as life seemed to come back to him. He would get sent home the next day. It was hard to believe that he was all but dead, and would bounce back as soon as he had the healing.

That happened several times, and the doctors could not explain it. He would be so bad that they would plan to send him to Hospice. I would pay him a visit and give him the healing, and the next day, again, he would be able to go home. I am not taking any credit for the healings, but I would like to think that his strong faith, belief in God, will to live, and my prayers of healing were helping him to hang in there.

He was back and forth, like that for several years, before his body wore out and God decided it was time to take him to the other side. He fought up until the end. His family, my sisters, Betty, Linda, June and I were there with him to say good-bye when he was called to the Spirit World. The morning he died, Mom, Marg, and Curly came to help him cross over. I sang the Church song, "In the Garden" to him to let him know that it was okay to go with God, and rest. Lou, told him he didn't need to worry anymore and it was okay to go. He died one month before his seventy-first birthday, and we know now that he isn't in pain anymore.

Chapter 19

It was around the time that Ruthie died, that Bob started acting as though he was more committed to me than he had ever been in the time we had been dating. He was more attentive and caring than I had known he could be, and I started getting closer to him. As I became closer to Bob, I could read his feelings and knew what he was going to do, even before he knew himself what he was doing. I knew he was going to ask me to marry him a long time before he even had any idea that he would. That information came to me through Spirit, and automatic writing. (Automatic writing is when a Spirit gives information through hand writing; sometimes in your handwriting, or sometimes in theirs.)

One day at work, a young woman that worked in the next department to me, asked if I had ever tried automatic writing. I told her that I had tried it before, but without any results. She showed me how she did it and told me to give it another try. She said that if you use a pencil rather than an ink pen, it seems to work better, then you need to relax and let your hand move as it wants. To my surprise, it seemed like it was working, but as usual, I was doubtful, until one of the other girls asked me to give her the answer to an important question. When I gave her the answer, plus some other information that was very accurate, it really surprised both of us. After that, when I started using automatic writing more, I began getting the information that Bob and I would be married. I started getting that message in the summer of 1991, but I found it hard to believe. I had also dreamed that we would marry, and of course, I wouldn't believe my dreams either.

Nevertheless, in September of 1992, for my birthday, Bob took me on a wonderful cruise. St. Thomas was one our stops, and that's where he bought me a beautiful ring with a large sapphire and baguette diamonds. Sapphires are my favorite stone, maybe, because they are also my birthstone.

Two days after we got back from the cruise, on his late father's birthday, I found out it was my engagement ring when he proposed to me. He told me the reason he did not propose to me while we were on the cruise, was because he wanted to do so on a day that was very special to him. That made me feel very good, since he was especially close to his father when he was alive.

Shortly after that, at the end of October, after discussing it with Bob and my doctor, I quit my job at the department store. Due to a fall at work, I had herniated a disc in my back and it was giving me many problems. I have had some serious health problems over the years, including cancer and (fibromyalgia - rheumatism.) This man of mine has his faults, like most people, but I give him credit for standing by me, and I love him for that.

Chapter 20

Shortly after I left the retail job, I started pursuing my Psychic work more, since I thought it would be easier for me than my old job. In doing so, I was asked to do some readings at the University of Toledo's main campus, here in town. The Student Union at U.T. put on the event for the students. It went over so well, that when I was finished there, they invited me to come over to their other campus to put on the same event for the Student Union, there. It went over equally as well, and there were so many students that wanted readings while I was there, they had to turn people away. They invited me to come back to do an annual Psychic program. Each time, I went back again, I read for some of the same students that I had seen before. They told me about some predictions that I made for them previously that had happened. There was a lady that I did a reading for that was very intense. I could see major problems for a male friend of hers. I felt there was something very wrong with his health, and that he was in great pain. She said, she hadn't seen him in a few days. I made her promise to find him because he needed her help. She asked me if I thought he was dead, and I told her, "No, but he needs your help, so please find him." I was there again the next day, and she stopped by and said that after calling a few friends, she found him. He had been shot and was now in the hospital, and she wanted to thank me for helping. It had turned out to be a good situation after all. It seemed that I had made a difference in someone's life just by being there. Along with that experience was another strange happening. I did a reading for a young lady that came in to see me who seemed very distressed. She was very interested in metaphysics and didn't know much about the subject, but would like to learn more. I asked her if she was having problems sleeping, because I felt worry with that. She admitted she was having problems sleeping and that she had been having bad dreams for about the past year. The dreams had started after she and some friends had been playing around with the Ouija board. She felt she had let a bad Spirit come through and it had been invading her dreams. She had awakened while fighting off a horrible thing. The nightmare had happened a couple of times in the past year, and she would wake up with scratch marks all over her. She was very upset and frightened, so I did the only thing that I knew to do, and that was to give her a healing. I said a prayer for God to send white light into her. After doing so, I cautioned her about the problems that can arise when using the Ouija board without protection.

I hope the prayer of healing has helped to bring peace back into her life. I also hope I was able to bring some light into all the other people that I read for while I was there. Doing the event for the students was really fun. They seem to get much enjoyment from it, and Dave, who arranged the program, was very helpful and kind. He is the person that made it possible for me to make all of the return visits to the University.

I had another strange occurrence happen on a return visit there. I did a reading for a young lady and her friend who was helping Dave put on the program. Later, as I was taking a break, the two young women came in and we were talking. They started asking me questions about how I became interested in the Psychic field. As I was telling them about how I began, I had a vision of a white haired old man. While I was describing him, I felt an extreme amount of love and warmth. His presence seemed to warm the whole room. The young lady said the description fit her grandfather, and that she had been very close to him before he died. He showed me an old yellow nylon sweater with brown buttons that was his favorite. She was amazed when I told her about the sweater, because it was true. He kept the sweater hidden in the trunk of his car, because no one wanted him to wear it. However, when he would take her to McDonald's to eat, he would take the sweater out and put it on, because it gave him great pleasure to wear it, and she agreed. I saw him smiling a lot, and it seemed that he was very pleasant to be around. The girl was very happy with the message.

After that, I did more readings for a couple more hours, in fifteen minute sessions. As I would get up to see the clients in and out, I noticed that my shoes kept coming untied several times. At first, I didn't really take notice, but then I found myself saying, "My darn shoes, especially my left one doesn't want to stay tied today."
I didn't remember having a problem with them before.
Later, as I was getting ready to leave for the day, I had a thought, and I asked the girl if her grandfather was mischievous. She said, he was a jokester and loved pulling little pranks on people to make them laugh.

I said aloud, "O.K. old man, you have had your fun and made me laugh, now behave yourself because I'm tired of tying my shoes." I sat down, rubbed my shoes together and did everything I could to get them to untie, but I couldn't make it happen. For the next three days that I was there, he made regular visits to do the untying bit, to bring a smile to my face. I had never tied my shoes so many times in such short time. Once in a great while, he still lets me know he is around, and I just smile and tell him to behave. It's good to know that people on the other side have a good sense of humor.

It seemed as though, since I had decided to get more involved with my Psychic work, it had been searching me out. Shortly after doing my work at the campus in town, I was asked to do some talks at Bowling Green University south of here where my daughter went to school. The students enjoyed my demonstrations so much that I was asked to return. It seemed, they had elected me to be the in-house Psychic.

The incident that I remember most from my readings down there, was about a young man who was very sad. He asked me to try and get a message from his father, who had been killed about five years before. I was able to receive a message from his father, and I felt an overwhelming sadness when I was giving it to him. The father wanted his son to know that he and his mother had to let him go, because they were keeping him from going on to where he was supposed to be. The young man agreed that they had not been able to let go. I could feel all the love that was holding his father back. The father said that his death had been fast and he didn't see who did it, but his head and ear were hurt. The son said that his father had been jumped from behind and had been shot in the head. I felt so bad for the young man, that shaking the feeling of pain and loneliness was hard for me to do. However, the man did tell me to tell his son that he would have a better Christmas that year than he'd had in quite sometime. I took that as, the boy and his mother would tell him good-bye, so he could cross over completely and begin learning what he was supposed to learn. I surely hope that message, in some way, helped the young man find some peace with his father's death. I carried a feeling of concern for the young man home with me, and I prayed that God would help him put some closure to his loss.

While doing the talks down at the University, I was surprised at how many young people that are interested in metaphysics. There was a good turnout for the programs and the students seemed to want to learn more about the subject, as they really enjoyed themselves. I wouldn't be surprised, if someday some of those students that attended would be writing a book about some of their strange experiences while developing their own Psychic ability.

One young lady, asked me what I thought about Ouija boards. I said, "I am afraid of them for anyone that doesn't realize what they are, and does not know enough to use Spiritual protection." Although, they are sold as games, I don't think they are a game that children or the unaware should play with, (but then, that's just my opinion.)

I have heard many stories of people having bad experiences while using the boards. I think there are lower Spirits, which are not Spiritually evolved and have bad intentions, just waiting for the opportunity to come through. If you don't know the difference between the lower and higher Spirits, and it can sometimes be hard to tell, and it can get very scary. The lower Spirits have been known to give false information. Even for someone trained on the subject, it can sometimes be hard to sort out the messages enough to know if they are coming from darkness or the light.

That young lady said that she and some friends had made contact with their girlfriend who had died, and her Spirit had given them information that only their friend would have known. It appeared that indeed, they had brought their friend through. By all means, if they should use the board again, I would advise them to please say a prayer of protection, and use the Spiritual white light before they begin.

Chapter 21

In pursuing my work in other ways, I was asked to be on a local radio talk show to discuss the Psychic realm. Corey, the host of the program, was a very funny and pleasant man. While he was preparing the equipment for the show. We were chit-chatting, and a woman came into my Psychic vision. When I described her, he thought it was his grandmother. She left a brief message and was gone. He asked me to give him a tarot reading on the air, and he was amazed at how accurate I was with the information I was giving him. Corey excitedly told over the air about the message that I had given him earlier from his grandmother.

Because of the radio show, I got a call from a man and his wife, who had lost their young daughter in an automobile accident. They wanted to know if I could contact her for them. I told them that I had been able to receive brief messages from Spirit, but I had never sat down to channel a whole reading from Spirit. So, for that reason, I couldn't promise any results. They wanted me to try anyway. I told them to bring something that was hers and that she had contact with, but again, I couldn't guarantee anything.

When they got to my apartment, it was as though their daughter walked through the door with them, because right away, I started getting goose-bumps. (That is what I feel when Spirit is around.)
It is my policy to do a reading one-on-one, so I asked the mother to sit down first. She brought her daughter's boom box to record the session. We had just begun the session when her recorder

started acting up. I asked the lady to see if her husband could fix it. He played around with it for a few seconds and it started working without him really doing anything to it. I told them that must be their daughter's way of getting Dad to sit in on the reading. So, I asked her father to join us.

The girl was very easy to communicate with. I told them about an old deserted house where she loved to go and spend time. While the daughter was there, she talked with the Spirit of an old woman who sat in a rocking chair. The parents confirmed later that the information was very true.

I mentioned the touch lamps in the house that kept coming on without reason, because she was playing games with them. I gave a description of the touch lamp in the girl's room, and exactly where it was located. I was able to give them details about their daughter, that made them realize it was she because there was no way I could know those things.

The girl was full of information to give her parents. She began to show me a vacuum sweeper in a room with a fireplace, and she said, "I hated that thing,"as she started laughing. When I told them these things, her mother laid her head down on the table and started crying hysterically. I looked at her father, and wondered what I had done wrong, but he said, "She's okay." After she calmed down, she explained that although the other things I had told them fit in place, she was just waiting for me to say something that she knew, I wouldn't have any way of knowing unless her daughter's Spirit told me what to say.

The story about the sweeper overwhelmed her. The mother was a neat freak. When the girl was alive and would have friends over or be watching television, Mom would drag out the sweeper and sweep the floor. Of course, it would upset the girl, but later, it became sort of a joke. The girl would throw pieces of lint on the floor, just to see how long it would take Mom to get out the vacuum and sweep up the mess. I communicated with the girl for about forty-five minutes, which is a long time to communicate with a Spirit, especially since it was the first time with her. Mom and Dad said she had been Psychic when she was alive, so maybe that's why she was so strong. I had to tell her to leave when her parents left.

That couple sent another couple to me. They belonged to the same support group, and I had similar results with bringing their daughter through. It was good to know that I was able to help them feel somewhat comforted, even if it was in a very small degree.

Chapter 22

Shortly after that, in late winter, some of my clients wanted me to give classes on Tarot. I had stomach and bowel problems, but I didn't know at the time just how serious it was. Nevertheless, I went ahead with the classes, although it wasn't easy for me health wise. I guess I did well, considering that I hadn't taught before. My students seemed impressed with my down to earth way of teaching. I didn't use a lot of fancy words they wouldn't understand, and I let them set the pace at which I taught. I just taught them the basics, which was really enough for them to get a good start. I told them that I wanted them to practice a lot with the cards on their own, so they could do some self-learning as well. When the classes were finished, my students asked me to give more in-depth classes later, when my health improved.

While I was still giving classes, around mid-March, I had a very strange occurrence happen to me. It had nothing to do with the classes, but it did interfere briefly, to some extent. In fact, it also interfered with my Psychic work. I was so absorbed in the situation, I even postponed readings. It was the first time, I had ever felt like I wasn't in control, and that was a feeling that I did not like at all. It seemed to be the only thing that I thought about or was interested in. It was causing problems between Bob and myself because I couldn't give him any time or attention. I found out later, that it was also affecting other people's relationships that were involved in the case. That was the only time, I have ever been frightened of my ability, and the only time I felt I wasn't in charge of the situation. I wasn't afraid of being harmed. I just felt I always needed to be in control, but that situation made me realize that I was going deeper into trance, than my guides and I had agreed on. I was used to having Spirit at my side giving information. Yet a few times, this Spirit was up front, and I was taking the back seat. Naturally, I didn't stand for that, long. Thank God, I only let that go on for less than two weeks. It all started one morning about four a.m., when Bob got home from work. He is a pressman for our local newspaper. He woke me up as he was getting into bed, and ask if I had heard about a young pilot that was missing from the area. I said, "No." Bob said that the young man was on his way to a nearby town in an adjoining state, to take his pilot's test, and had disappeared on the way there. A local Psychic told the authorities that she felt he went down in Wagoner's Lake. The moment he said that, I became more awake, and without knowing why, I said, "She's completely off base, he's not where he is supposed to be. I see him lying on a ledge, just before the end of the Earth. There's a big drop off before a large lake, and the drop off is dark and mucky; I see that the thumb is very important."

I couldn't go back to sleep, and when I got up in the morning, I knew that I had to tell the Police about this, even if they didn't believe me. The Police directed me to a lady named Colleen, the manager of the airport that he was supposed to have flown to for the test. Since she was working on the case, I told her about the information that I had acquired that morning. As I was talking to her, I was getting more information. I described the young man's approximate age and appearance. She told me I was correct. I had no previous knowledge of what he looked like, since I hadn't seen the paper. It was several days later that I finally saw his picture, and I looked at it with reluctance, because I didn't in any way, want to have any interference with my impressions. But looking at the picture only made the information come in stronger. That first morning that I spoke with Colleen I started getting lots of goose-bumps, and I told her I thought he was dead. She informed me that she had some Psychic ability herself, so she believed the things that I was saying. In fact, she seemed to be picking up some of the same feelings that I did. She said, that the information I was giving made sense and fit in. She also knew some of the information that I was giving her, were things that I wouldn't have any knowledge of because it was terms that only a pilot would use. I saw two roads close together. With them, I got the numbers, twenty-two, and twenty-three, but twenty-three seemed to stick in my mind that it was very important. Colleen and I talked back and forth for a day and a half, and each time that we spoke, I would give her more information. I felt the information was coming directly from the young man, whose name was Jeff. On the second day, Jeff told me that Colleen wasn't relaying the information to the appropriate people fast enough. He said that I needed to call someone else. Apparently, Colleen told the Air Patrol about my phone call because later that day, I got a call from a Colonel, who was in charge of that organization. He said he would have Les, who was in charge of the case, call me back before the day was over. Les told me later when he called, that the reason it took longer to get back with me, was because he asked the State Police to do check on me. He needed to see if I was for real, even though he knew that the information I had given was too accurate and uncanny to be a hoax. I found out that he had Psychic experiences before, and he was a believer, so it made it easier to work with him. He seemed like a very nice and considerate man, and he was very easy to talk to. In fact, he was too easy to talk to, because I found out right away that he was able to put me into a deeper trance than I was comfortable with. There were many telephone calls back and forth, between Les and myself. Each time I would get any new information, I would call him. There seemed to be such an urgency with the information that Jeff was sending through to me. It was as though I was obsessed with finding him.

I recall the first day that I talked with Les and gave him all the information that I had received. He called back later to see if I had come up with anything more. That time, he kept me on the telephone for about four hours and had me in and out of a semi-deep trance most of that time. Even though, I was in trance pretty deep, I still felt that I knew what was going on around me. I know, I was describing places and things that I had never seen before and it all made sense to Les. I described the place where the young man was lying. He wasn't in the plane when it landed in some mucky water at the edge of a large lake. They had people out looking for him, and they were using my clues as they searched. When Les would ask me to center in, he would start directing his conversation to Jeff, and that would be when I felt myself taking the back seat and Jeff would answer the questions. Some things that I said seemed very strange, because most of the information that came from my mouth made no sense to me at all, but it did to Les. He told me, that when I would center in, I took on a completely different tone of voice and personality. When the search crew was out searching, I was giving clues as to where Jeff's body was. I could actually look up and see the planes searching overhead so clearly, that I was able to describe what one looked like, and who was in it. Les said my description was correct. I gave them the name of one of the search groups, and I described some of the men that were in the group. One person had body odor and one was nearby smoking a cigarette. Jeff complained of the offensive body odor and smoke. I asked what a bull was doing out there, and Les admitted that all of these things were checked out and confirmed. The bull turned out to be one of the searchers that looked like Bull from television's "Night Court." Les was amazed when I described, in detail, the emblem on the front of the group leader's shirt. We both felt that the young man was dead, but he didn't know it. Les asked me how I would make him realize it, and I said that when the time came, I would tell him.

I felt, if they had applied all of the clues that Jeff was giving them, they should have found him. Jeff felt the same way, and was getting very frustrated with them. He said that they were not paying attention, and they were right on top of him, but weren't seeing him. I could clearly see in my vision where he was, as though I was up in the air looking down at the area, and it seemed to match all the other information I was getting.

In one of the sessions, he said they were only ten minutes, or ten miles, or ten something from him. At that time, I had many mixed feelings, of anticipation, happiness, warmth, but then complete disappointment, and loneliness, because they had passed by the area where he was. When I mentioned the warm feeling, it was at the same time that his father was said to be searching very close to the area where he was. The next day, after all that information didn't help find him, Les called and said he wanted to ask more questions. He told me to center in on Jeff, and that's all it took. Les started to ask questions about the plane, and what happened. It seemed like, I was driving an airplane. It was a very tight space, and I kept rubbing my right knee and thigh, as if they were sore. With my left arm, I kept making a motion of swinging my arm out to my left, and then back in toward my side. I kept doing that in a rhythm motion, like I was controlling something.

Then Jeff said that it was starting to get rough up there, and it was really bumpy. The instrument on the right was getting worse. The instrument was pointing at 400, and I felt like I was in a terrible spin that was going downward, and everything turned dark. The last thing that Jeff said was, "OH GOD!" in an awful cry. That was a very scary feeling. I truly believe I crashed an airplane, and I don't have any desire to ever go through that again. I told Les that day, I didn't want to go that deep into trance again. After that incident, it was as though Jeff backed off some, and I was able to feel normal again. It seemed like the urgency wasn't as extreme, and I didn't feel as obsessed as before, with finding him. I think he and I came to an understanding that day, that I had done about all I could do and the rest was up to the authorities. Les asked me to go up in a helicopter with the crew, to see if I could recognize the area that I had described, but I refused, because of the fear of height, especially after the plane crash incident. We arranged a meeting with Colleen, Les, the Colonel, and myself. I gathered up the maps and notes with all the other information, and put them in a folder. On the drive up there, Jeff and I made an agreement, that when I turned all of the information over to those people, he would leave me alone, because he knew I had done all that I could do. When I walked in, I handed them the folder, and told them Jeff said that was all the information they needed to find him, if they would just pay attention. Many times through it all, he told me they weren't paying attention. Colleen, the airport manager was not able to attend but there were other people there besides the ones that I expected to see. I was there for about five hours, and went over everything that they needed to go over. Then Les asked me if I would go into trance one last time, but I told him that I really wasn't comfortable with that. So, he said, "well lets just sit and talk, and see if anything more comes out." They started to ask questions, and then Les said there's something that we need to do. I told him, that he already knew, and had known since I crashed the plane with him. Les had been very concerned all along, that Jeff would have to be told he was dead. He said he needed to be sure, and all he had to say was, "Center in on Jeff," and there he was. While I was in trance, I told them about an old dead tree that was nearby, with some other landmarks and people. I said that the reason they couldn't see him was, that he was on a layered ledge that was sort of hidden like a cave.

Then Les asked Jeff to tell them where he was. It seemed as though I was in the plane, and a very bright light was at my left shining through the window. Les asked, "What do you look like?" Hesitation.
Again, "How do you look?" Pause.
Again, "When you look at yourself what do you see?"
It seemed like I was sitting way up high and had to look over and way down.
I said, "I see a big mass of white light."
Les said, "What is it?"
I said, "I guess it's me, I can't see anything else."
With those words, though my eyes were closed, tears streamed down my face, as I felt an extreme sadness.
Les said, "Judy, you can come back now."
When I opened my eyes, I felt like my stomach was going in circles. I was more drained than I had ever felt before while doing any Psychic work.

I don't know if I gave any information while I was in trance that I can't remember. However, someone came in later and said the dead tree was where I had said it was. They told me that the numbers twenty-two and twenty-three were the page numbers on their flight map of the area I had given them to search, and the information was more on page twenty three. Those numbers seemed to pop up many times in strange ways, that day. The next day, they used all of my information to search, and said they didn't find anything. They had made a decision; if they didn't find him that day they were going to discontinue the search, because they had exhausted the funds and manpower.

After that, I tried to call Les to see if anything more had come up. He said there was not any news, and that it was time to give it up and go on with our lives. He also told me that the search had caused relationship problems for many people working on the case, because they had been putting so much effort, time, and energy into it.

He said he was going to write a letter of thanks and recommendation for me, just in case I wanted to help with any future cases. I told him he didn't need to do that, but he insisted. He must have gotten too busy to write the letter, because there wasn't anymore communication from him.

I also tried to call Colleen at the airport, several times, but she never returned my calls. I definitely felt deceit coming from that direction, but couldn't understand exactly what it was all about.

A couple months later, I called Jeff's father and told him about all that had transpired. I asked if his son had been found, and he said he hadn't. I offered him the same information that I had given the authorities. He said he had detectives working on the case, and he would have one call me in the next day or so, but no one ever called. I still felt like I had left something unfinished, so I put all the information in an envelope and mailed to his house. Still, no response.

To this day, I can't understand the situation. As far as I know the case is still unsolved. I find it hard to believe that the information I received, could be anything but real, because it was so overpowering. As time passes, I often wonder if the information that I received was from Jeff, or some other pilot's Spirit.

Chapter 23

After that, at the beginning of summer, as I was getting back to normal with my life, I found out I had a polyp on my colon. When they removed it, they found out it was cancer. That had been the reason for all the health problems I was having when I had been doing the Tarot classes.

I began giving myself healings at that time, and I truly believe they helped. The doctor thought he had gotten all of the cancer when he removed the polyp, but they couldn't be completely sure. I felt they had gotten it all, but the doctors and all of my family wanted me to have that part of my colon removed, to be sure. I decided that I should go ahead and have the surgery, so I could be cured.

Bob wanted to marry me before the surgery, so we got married the month before. It was a bright summer day when the wedding took place. It was outside, by the pond, at the same park where we went on our first date. It was a small ceremony, with just family and a few friends. After the ceremony, we had a pool party, in the backyard of our home, with food and fun to celebrate our special day.

The surgery went as planned, and was a great success. I was right, they had gotten all of the disease before. I am now cured. Thank God, for my wonderful doctors and the thorough job that they did. The next morning, after the surgery, I had a long walk to get to the shower because there wasn't one in my room. Though, I was a little weak and very sore, I wasn't about to let it keep me down. I kept giving myself healings, and the doctors were amazed at my speedy recovery. My primary care doctor came in two days after my surgery, while two of my sisters were there. He said to them,

"Can you believe how fast she has bounced back?" My reply was, "What was I supposed to do, just lie there?"

He said, "No, but people usually don't bounce back this fast, after colon surgery."

I told him, it was because I had been working on myself with healings. I truly believe that prayer and self-healing made all the difference, along with my belief in God's great healing power.

Chapter 24

I went back to my apartment after my surgery, instead of Bob's home, so I could concentrate on my recovery. I felt it would be better for me, not having to deal with moving then, especially into a place that wasn't the familiar surroundings that I was used to.

I also knew I would have to learn to get used to Bob's two big sheep dogs, Megan and Rambo, who are sister and brother, and his cat, Chester. I'm not an animal person, but I did have a cat named Boots. She was old, and I knew she would have a hard time adjusting to the other animals, and I wasn't well enough to deal with the stress. I knew I would have to adjust to the responsibility of the animals, since they could be more work than children could. If nothing else, I was sure I would learn a lot of tolerance.

Yet, shortly after I started to recover more, we moved into my new husband's house. Vicki had just graduated from college, and decided to live with us for the time being. She was hoping to save up her money, until she could get enough funds together to leave town for bigger and better places. Hopefully, by doing so it would help her to pursue a job in her field of study.

(My dream is, that one day in the not so far future, I can pick up a high fashion magazine, and see my daughter's name, "VICTORIA," in large print as one of the top fashion designers.)

I am sure it will happen because she wants very much to make something of her career. She surly has been my strength and purpose through the years.

I have my office in the basement of our house, and it is quite homey and comfortable. I have some beautiful Native American articles and pictures on the walls and shelves. Some have been given to me by Bob, Vicki, family, friends, and clients. I have several Native American collector's plates on the wall, that my daughter has given to me on different occasions. Vicki is a great gift-giver, and I adore the plates that she is collecting for me. She also buys other Native American odds and ends for me. I have several crystals that she, Bob, and some clients have helped me to acquire. The crystals are a source of energy and healing. I have a large ceramic figure of an Indian that was given to me by my oldest sister Gertie, whom I don't get to see very often. One summer, I went down to visit her on her farm in Southern Ohio. It made my day when she took me upstairs in her old farmhouse to find him for me.

My office is where I spend much of my time, and even when I am not reading for clients, it's my getaway, to spend time by myself. When I am in my office, I feel it is my own little space where I can be me, especially when I am working with my computer. It has become a special friend to me, because I can feed it all my thoughts, and feel comfortable doing so. That brings to mind a strange incident that happened with my computer. I decided to do some writing, and in doing so, I went back to add more to where I had already written. As I was adding the information, I stopped with the words "I am," because I had to go upstairs. When I came back to pick up where I left off, "am" had turned into "Sam." I had a hard time trying to delete Sam but when I finally did, I asked, "Sam who?" He said, Sam Jacobs, and he showed me a vision of himself as an old man, while saying he had a lot of knowledge to share. I think he is helping write this book: when I began, I could hardly type, but when I am writing, I zip right along. I wonder, "Is he the shoe string culprit?"

Chapter 25

I took two months off from my Psychic work after my surgery, and then, when I got settled in at my new home, I resumed. Some of my regular clients told me to let them know when I was ready to start doing readings again, and I did. It kept me quite busy trying to catch up, but it felt good to be back at my work.

One of those regulars was Freda. She was a very pleasant young lady from Venezuela. I had a call from her one-day, and she said I had been a lot of help to her. She told me that the things I had seen for her had come about. I was happy that I had helped her when she needed my advice.

She told me I had a "witch mouth," and when I asked her to explain, she said that all the things I told her had come true. Laughing, she said that was what she would say to her mother, because she was usually right when she said things were going to happen.

I kept warning Freda of an unexpected pregnancy if she didn't take precaution. She did not heed the warning, so she now has three little ones close in age. Even though, she loves them dearly, she really has her hands full trying to keep up with them.

Another one of my regulars, whose name is Rita, was also anxious for me to get back to work. She said, I had been able to give her much help with my readings over the years. I was her first experience with a Psychic, when I first went professional. She has kept a diary of my readings and goes back and reads it from time to time. I have made many predictions that came about for her, including the one when I told her that her father was not well. I thought he would leave her an inheritance from insurance, which would be a large sum of money. Rita couldn't understand that, because she knew her mother would do good just to have enough insurance to bury him. Her father died not long after that, and his death was blamed on a procedure that the doctor was thought to have messed up. Her mother is now suing the doctor and the hospital, for the wrongful death of her husband, and Rita's name is listed along side hers on the lawsuit. I imagine the insurance inheritance will be from malpractice insurance. I also told her she would inherit a house, and that is about to happen, thanks to her mother's love and kindness.

I would like to mention another one of my clients whose name is Mary. The first time she called me, she said she was ready to bottom out, because her husband had just died and she was having a hard time adjusting. She didn't know anything about Psychics, and didn't really believe they were for real. When she heard me on a radio show, she was compelled to call me. She sounded so desperate when she asked for a reading that I scheduled her for the next day. She said she had second thoughts about coming, while driving here. She came a skeptic and left a believer. In the first reading her husband Art came through so strong that he gave me the usual goose-bumps on my arms. I told her about circumstances around his death, and that he was still around her. He wanted her to stop blaming herself, because she had done everything possible to keep him comfortable during his years of illness. He asked me describe him to her and tell her his little quirks and his great sense of humor, which Mary confirmed. There were things he said he wanted done pertaining to his mother and granddaughter. I gave her important information that became very useful, about her work, finances, and personal life.

I was then able to tell her about her new man that she was going to be meeting, and Art was going to be instrumental in bringing that into being. He could see how lonely and upset she was and he didn't want her to feel that way, so he was going to help her. The man he was sending to take care of her would be very good for her, and she wouldn't be lonely and sad anymore. I described the new man's appearance and mannerisms. She met the man, whose name is Jack, shortly after that. When she met him, it was so uncanny, because he looked so much like my description, her knees turned to rubber. They hit it off from the start, and began seeing each other. Although, there were problems in the relationship, I was able to help her see them in advance, so she could find solutions. In another reading, Art kept telling me to have her look for an insurance policy. It was an old policy, and it meant money for her. It came up at every subsequent reading, and she had no idea what he was talking about. Later, when Art's mother died, Mary found out that it was his insurance policy that was about fifty years old, and his mother had changed it after his death, to make Mary the beneficiary. Later, I informed her that she and Jack would marry, and I thought September would be a good time for the event. Recently, she said they were getting married next September but I don't know if she remembered that I predicted it for then. There were many times that she thought my predictions were wrong, but with time, and seeing them come about she admitted that she was the one that was wrong.

Another prediction that I made turned out to be a financial blessing for Jodi, who was another one of my steady clients. I told her I felt her father would leave a lot of money when he passed over. She was doubtful about that, since she wasn't close to her father. She didn't think he would leave her anything because he never did anything for her while he was alive. As it turned out, he died and left Jodi, her sister, and two brothers several thousands of dollars each. She was really surprised and grateful. I must say, she deserved it more than some people, because she is a hard worker and a good person as well as a good mother. She is the only person I know that no matter when you ask her how she is, she always says she can't complain. Her not complaining paid off for her with a financial blessing.

Speaking of predictions, reminds me of an experience that happened concerning my niece Cindi's friend. One evening, Cindi called me on the telephone and asked me if I would help a friend of hers that needed some advise. She said her friend's husband, who was a truck driver, had been missing for four days and no one knew where he was. It was on the television news, but they hadn't had any luck finding him. I asked Cindi if he wasn't someplace with another woman, and she said she didn't think so. I told her to have her friend call me. Her friend called me immediately and I sat down to do a reading for her. I saw that her husband was not in this area but he was not really far away, and he was near water. I was sure he wasn't harmed and was with a woman. She would hear from him either that night or the next day and he would come back home. I saw him being confused, and his boss knew where he was. That evening on the eleven o'clock news, I heard that the truck driver had been found in Cleveland, which is by water and not that far from here. After watching the news, I called the lady and asked her if she had seen the news, and she had. After she had talked to me, she called his boss and he admitted that her husband was in Cleveland. He had talked with him, he sounded confused and he was with another woman. She got a phone call from her husband later that evening saying he was coming home.

One day, a girl named Mira, who worked with my daughter, came over for a reading. I saw that she was going to be getting a new job soon and it had something to do with cars. There would be a trip for her that was connected to the job. I thought she would win a cruise because the trip would be over water. It looked like a very happy time for her. She told me when I was done, that she had come to see if she would win a contest that she entered for a job. It was doing TV commercials for a place that installed car sound systems. She was very happy when I said it looked very good. She told Vicki later to tell me that she won the contest, and she didn't know before hand that part of the winnings was a cruise. She had a great time on the cruise, and when she came back she did the commercial. She did a good job with it, and was very excited that it had happened just as I had predicted.

There is a story that I talk about often, concerning a prediction that I made for one of my few male clients whose name is Gabe. He came to me one day very distressed. He said that he and his wife were having problems and he needed help. I told him that I didn't think they would get a divorce because I still saw them together. I thought they might separate for a brief time, but I didn't really feel they would be apart. I felt a lot of love between them and I saw them together. He came back again and said they were separating, and again, I saw them together. I couldn't understand why the cards kept showing them together. He said, he had been to other readers and they all told him they would get a divorce and never be together again. I still felt they would be together. He came back again and said they got a divorce. I was totally confused, because again the cards told me they were together. I apologized for being wrong, and told him I didn't understand because even though I am subject to mistake, I could still see them together. By that time, I was really starting to feel very uncertain about my ability. I didn't even want to read for the man again

102

because it was upsetting for me to see the turmoil he was in. The cards were telling me things that weren't happening to them. I don't know why he kept coming back to me, because I wouldn't have if I had been in his shoes. I finally told him to get some counseling and to back off and let his wife make the moves. She didn't like to be pushed into anything. The counseling would prove that he was making a good effort, and if he would leave her alone they would be together. Four years later, Gabe called me. I hadn't heard from him for awhile and he sounded better than I had ever heard him. He thanked me and said he would never forget me, because of all the readers he had gone to, I was the only one that gave him hope and the encouragement to be patient. He and his ex-wife had gotten back together. They were still in love and going to remarry. They were also planning to have another child. He said, neither one of them had dated anyone else while they had been separated, and it was as though they had never been apart. So, that was probably why I had still seen them together; it made my day to hear the news.

Another prediction that I made was for Loreen, who is also one of my regular clients and one that I mentioned earlier when I was discussing healings. In a reading that I did for her, I saw a single yellow rose in a vase sitting on a glass top table, but I was not sure what it meant. In another reading, I told her not to worry about money because she had an inheritance coming that would be a big help to her financially. As I continued on with the reading, I saw problems with her daughter who lived down South, and was a second Lieutenant in the Army. I felt she was hurt or ill, and I encouraged Loreen to go to see her. There was something definitely wrong but Spirit wouldn't let me see what it was. (I have learned from doing readings over the years, that when there is going to be a death for someone close to the client; my Guides shut me down and won't let the message come through clearly. I always get an upset but foggy feeling, and they quickly move me on to another phase in the reading. That is their way of keeping their agreement to not let me see really bad things.) Loreen went to visit her daughter and came back to report that she was fine, which was a big relief for me. A few months later, Loreen got the news that her daughter was killed in an automobile accident. She was extremely upset, but she was glad that I had told her to go see her daughter earlier, otherwise, she wouldn't have gotten to see her before she died. She realized, at her daughter's funeral, what the yellow rose meant that I had seen about a year before. When she walked into the room where they were showing her daughter, her attention was brought to a single yellow rose on a glass table next to her daughter's casket. The rose was from the people that her daughter baby-sat for when she was younger.

I advised Loreen, at the time of her daughter's death, that she shouldn't trust her ex-husband because he was being deceitful. He was trying in a round about way, to get her to sign off as her daughter's co-executrix to her estate. At the time, Loreen couldn't see any reason why she shouldn't do as he wanted, but I felt he was up to no good. Later, she told me, she was glad she listened to me and heeded the warning about signing off her daughter's estate. Otherwise, she would have lost a large sum of money from the inheritance. The Army had a large insurance policy on her daughter that Loreen was unaware of. Her ex-husband intended to get her share, and that was what the deceit was about. After everything was settled, I informed her that there was another insurance policy, and to keep looking for it. She kept looking until she found another small policy.

(There have been several different occasions when I have seen insurance policies for people, that they were not aware of until I insisted they look for them, and they were able to find them.) Several times, as I was doing readings for her, I saw a lot of deceit with some people that she worked with, including her boss. At the time, Loreen was running for some sort of public office in her county. I told her that she had a very good chance at winning, except for a deceitful situation between her female boss that she was running against, and a man that was also part of the campaign. I could see that it was a big mess that would blow up in their faces one day, and be in the newspapers. It took several years to come about, but Loreen sent me copies of the newspaper articles of the people that I had mentioned and they were being prosecuted for wrong-doings. She was really excited when she called to tell me, she wanted me to see the newspaper articles of the situation that I had predicted for her about five years prior.

I had a call one day from a lady named Linda, who hadn't been to see me for a couple of years. She said so much of her reading had come true that she needed another one. I had told her that she would be moving to another house and someone else would pay for it. She thought it would be really strange if it happened. Certain events took place and a relative that was handicapped ended up needing her help. He moved in with Linda and her husband, because he had no one else to take care of him. It turned out to be his money that I had seen helping with the move. Linda reminded me that she had brought a female friend with her when she had been to see me before. She proceeded to tell me that I had told her friend that she was going to leave her husband. Her friend and her husband were getting along just fine, so they couldn't understand how that could take place. They joked about it when they left my house. Less than a year later, her friend found out she had bone cancer and died. Linda said it was strange that I had not seen her friend's death. I brought up the fact that it was my Guide's way of protecting me.

Chapter 26

If you recall, previously, I did a prediction for my old associate Beth, about the dark featured man that she would be meeting and she unbelievingly said, "Yeah, right." It was a few years later before it came about, but it turned out exactly as I had predicted.

Beth met her dream man through her sister, who worked with him. He has dark features, a black sports car, and a great job that lets him travel all over the world. Beth is now married to a wonderful guy, whose name is Duane. They have a lovely new home, and she is pregnant with their first child, that I think is a girl.

In fact, she had me over to their house to do a Psychic party for some of her friends. We had a good time, and the girls seemed excited that I was able to give them some important information. One of the guests was Angie, whom had been Beth's friend for years, and who used to work with us. I had never read for her before, and she was excited about the reading. Beth and Angie asked me to do a seance for them at a later date. (A seance is channeling Spirit for more than one person at one time.)
I told them I didn't have a lot of experience with seances, but I would give it a try. They would let me know when they were available so we could make plans.

As time passed, I was communicating more with Spirit, and it was getting easier to do so. It was common to be talking to someone and receive Spirit messages for them. Some time passed, and Beth contacted me to follow through with the plans to do the seance. It was a rare occasion for me to sit down to do a seance for a group of people. Beth, Angie, and two of their friends were present. I was a little hesitant, because I was not sure how it would turn out. Beth's friend, Julie, wanted to have the seance at her house because she felt her dead brother's Spirit was there. I agreed to do it there, with the condition that I would have a room with complete privacy and no distractions. When I got there, I found that they didn't provide a room with no distractions, but instead, wanted me to perform it in Julie's parent's kitchen. There were wall to wall windows that looked out over the lake and a boat dock near by, which was very distracting. Julie's small son was sleeping in a nearby bedroom with the dog. I was concerned that he would wake up and come out and be frightened. One of her brothers that lived nearby popped in and would likely do so again. She was afraid that he wouldn't be too understanding of us having a seance in their kitchen. I told them, that I couldn't do a seance there, because there were just too many possible distractions. I don't think they realized what a serious undertaking it was. I informed them that I could be harmed if I was startled while going into trance deeper than I planned, which could possibly happen. At first, they said they understood, but after awhile, they talked me into giving it a try. I said I would, but I didn't have any intention of going into any kind of deep trance state. I wasn't comfortable doing it and couldn't relax knowing the possible interruptions. It didn't turn out as well as I had hoped, because of the circumstances, but I did better than I thought I would considering all the obstacles. I would like to tell about some Spirit messages that I received during the seance. I was able to bring Julie's brother in, but he was hesitant because he wanted his mother around to hear the message. He definitely was present, and I was able to give her some information from him, but her grandfather was around her even stronger. Julie's grandfather showed me what he looked like, so I could describe him and let her know who he was, and she agreed with the description. He was teasing about a dress his wife wore often, and he did not like it. He kept talking about the quilts his wife made. He showed her lying in bed, and covered with a quilt that was made with lots of loud colors on it. He said he watches her sleep, because he gets a kick out of watching her sleep with that busy quilt. He also showed the gorgeous headboard of the bed that had posts and was dark brown. Julie said her grandmother made quilts, and she had made a couple with loud colors that were not pretty. She did look weird, all covered up in her busy quilt in the bed that was dark brown and had posts. Grandpa showed me the old house that they lived in, with all the intricate woodwork on the outside that made it very beautiful. When I described it to Julie, she recognized it, along with the special brown rocking chair that he used to sit in on the porch and the white fence around the yard. There were many beautiful pieces of very old furniture in the house. He mentioned something about a brother, who had reddish-color hair that wasn't well. Then, he was talking about knowing someone that lived in a very large white house, whom I presumed to be his brother. Julie confirmed all of the information that he had given me. He said Julie's mother was going to be getting a gorgeous ring, soon, for a special occasion that was coming up. It had baguette diamonds, and a large blue stone in the center. Julie laughed, and said her parent's anniversary was coming up. Before he left for vacation, her father asked her to go and pick out a ring for her mother. She said it would have baguette diamonds and an emerald. I ask her if Grandpa was color blind, because he showed me a blue stone, and she said he was, at that. She thought she might not be able to find the emerald she wanted, and might have to get a sapphire instead. Grandpa really seemed to have a sense of humor because he kept saying funny things. Julie was going to send her parents on a trip for their anniversary. I felt the trip would be delayed, because I didn't feel anything in the works. She hadn't made the arrangements yet, so maybe that was it, but I thought there would be other delays. I ran into Julie's mother later and she told me that she and her husband had gone on the cruise; they had a great time. She saw a beautiful ring with a blue stone and just had to have it. Her husband bought it for her. She was surprised when I told her Grandpa had told me about it in his message to her daughter. The only delay that she knew about was that her son and his wife were supposed to go along, but they backed out at the last minute.

I received a message for Josie, one of the other ladies that was there. The message was from a girl that looked very much like her, and I felt it was her sister. The girl said her mother had a miscarriage, she was the result, and was Josie's sister. She had a lot of light around her, which meant that she was in good hands, and had learned her lessons well in the Spirit World. She wanted Josie to know that she has the ability to draw and is very creative, even if she doesn't know it. Her sister is going to help her bring it out and use it. She showed me a little boy with red hair, and about two or three years old. We couldn't figure out who he was. I asked Josie if she had a son that plays sports, because I saw a small boy sitting on a bench. There were girls on his team, and he didn't really like the team. She admitted that she did have a son who played soccer with girls on the team. The little red haired boy was somehow connected to her son, and maybe soccer. I described the color of her son's cap, and said that he never took it off, and she agreed. She said her son wanted a brother, so I felt the boy was the brother that was coming in, but it would be in a couple of years.

There was a message for Angie who was present, and a woman came through for her, by the name of Rose, or Rosa. To clarify who she was, she showed me a piece of material with roses on it. The only person that Angie could recognize with that name, was Sister Rose Angell. She was a nun at the school Angie had gone to when she was younger. The nun was very fond of Angie when she was going to school. Sister Rose showed me curtains with roses at a kitchen window, and Angie said that is what she has. I asked Angie if she knew she was getting a new bracelet, and she said she had been wanting a tennis bracelet. I felt, she would be changing her mind and getting a different kind. I saw a gold one about a half-inch wide that had fancy workings and looked very beautiful.

There was also a message for Beth that evening, from her brother Carl, who had supposedly committed suicide several years before. He came through and gave her the same message that he previously had given me to relay to her. He showed me that he was out in the wilderness, camping. He was sitting by a campfire relaxing, or maybe just warming himself, because I didn't really see him cooking or eating anything.

I kept saying the girlfriend did it, and Beth thought I meant his ex-girlfriend, because she had a lot to gain from his insurance policies that he had in her name. I told her it wasn't the old girlfriend, but the current one. Beth's brother had called home before he died, and said that he had broken up with his long-time girlfriend. He also said that he was going to change his will and leave everything he owned to Beth.

Shortly after that, he turned up missing, and it was about a year before they found what little was left of his remains. The authorities supposedly confirmed it was him from dental records, and they cremated his remains without an autopsy. It seemed to me, that there were too many things they didn't have answers to, like why was Beth's father's name instead of her brother's, on the death certificate? The police said Carl shot himself in the head with a rifle, but that didn't fit the vision that he showed to me. As he was sitting by the fire, I could see two people standing behind him. There was a female with blond hair and a man with dark hair and a beard. Neither of them looked well kept.

I felt the man was a lover to the woman who was the so-called girlfriend to Beth's brother. Carl said that she had asked him for money, but he didn't have any because it was back at the house. When he didn't come up with any money, the man got angry and hit Carl over the head with a large rock. All he showed me then, was darkness and silence. There wasn't any noise from a gun. Carl said some people were camping over to his right, and a young woman there had seen the whole thing but was afraid to say anything about it.

He also showed me two trucks that were parked nearby. They were along side a river or lake. One was a black 4x4 and the other was a red pick-up truck. Beth said that she thought her brother owned a truck that was red.

I wish they hadn't burned his remains, because they might have detected the hit on the back of the head. They would have known by the bump that he didn't kill himself. I wish there was some way they could find out for sure, so she and her family could have some sort of final closure on the matter. Carl has been gone for a few years, and Beth has really had a hard time dealing with it. It was upsetting when he came through the second time with the same information as before, because it forced her to realize that he might really be gone forever.

She is still very sensitive about her brother and all that happened. She has never really accepted his death. I wish she could find the closure that she needs to be able to cope with the loss of a loved one.

Chapter 27

The messages from the Spirit World seemed to be coming stronger and more frequent as I did my work. I would like to share some more of these messages that I found to be very interesting.

One day, my sister Linda, brought two ladies that she worked with over for a reading. Before we even got down to my office, one of the ladies' mother's Spirit came to me and wanted to give her daughter a message. I thought she would be the one that I would read for first. Somehow, it happened that the other lady wanted to be first. By the time I got to her friend, her mother's message had disappeared. The only thing I was able to remember was that she had appeared briefly and was gone. Maybe, the reason I forgot was that when I was reading for the first lady, she had a Spirit visitor that came through very strong and clear.

She was a nurse at a nursing home and I asked her if she had worked with a young man in his teens; he had brown hair, deeper color skin and he called her Mommy. She said she had taken care of a young black boy that had a crippling disease, and they had become very close before he passed over. "Yes, he did call her Mommy," because she used to pick him up and take him to her house to visit. She used to treat him as if he were part of her family. I could feel much love coming from him for her as he was giving the message. There was other information that I gave to her from him that made sense to her. She told my sister that I had told her things that there was no way I could have known about.

She doesn't know that I have lots of help and guidance from my Spirit Helpers in the Spirit World.

One of my regulars that has been coming to me for years, was a very nice lady named Vanessa. She has always given me positive feed back about how well I read for her, and all of the information that I have given her over the years. She said she doesn't make any important decisions without consulting me first. I told her that she shouldn't put so much emphasis on the information that I gave to her, because I am subject to mistake. She insisted she had that much trust in me. It has been scary for me to know that I could influence someone's life in such a way. It really puts me on the spot, because I wouldn't want to steer her or anyone else in the wrong direction. My job surely has had a lot of responsibility attached to it. She has sent two of her daughters, a sister, some friends, and several people that she works with to see me. They all say that Vanessa thinks I'm the greatest and she has much respect for my work. One of Vanessa's daughters named Nita, also became one of my regulars. She has a bubbly personality like her mother. I had an interesting thing happen once, when I was doing a reading for Nita that involved Spirit. A young man that was a friend of hers, appeared with a message. I had just begun the reading, when the young man came through and started talking about the color blue. I described him to her and she said that it was Dickey, a friend of hers that had just died a few days before. He kept talking about the color blue, and began laughing about a dumb blue suit that they had buried him in. Nita confirmed the color of the suit. He seemed to have a sense of humor, because he kept joking around. She said he had been very funny when he was here on Earth. He brought up the fact about something being wrong with the red car. It was then that I realized, he was telling me he had died in a car accident. Nita confirmed that the information was correct. He seemed to have very loving feelings for a baby that was very important to him. I thought she was his at first, but then he said it was his buddy's, and he played with her a lot. He mentioned the letter J, who was his buddy Josh, and the baby's father. There was an argument that he had with his girlfriend just before he died, and he thought it was a big joke. Nita said he and his girlfriend had been fighting, but they were supposed to make up the next day. He wanted to tell his girlfriend not to feel bad about the fight, nor be sad, because he had an easy transition over. He came through really strong and got his message over very clear. Nita felt much better when she found out that he was okay; she was very happy to receive a message from him.

One day, Vanessa brought a woman that she worked with, over for a reading. Once in a great while, I would do a reading that was very disturbing to me. Although most of them were on a positive note, sometimes I would get a person that was hard to read for. When I looked at the woman's cards, I had a very dreadful feeling. The turmoil and distress was so profound that I couldn't sort out what I was supposed to tell her. There have only been a couple of times that I have looked at the cards and saw total confusion; to the point of feeling like I was in a fog and can't sort out what they mean. I grappled my way through the reading the best I could, and was glad when her time was up. I don't remember any information that I gave her, except, I do remember telling her that everything would be okay, in time. I felt really bad that I wasn't able to help her more that I did. Shortly after that, I realized why I had such sadness reading for her. Vanessa told me, the lady's daughter had suddenly died, and the woman ended up in a mental hospital for a short time. She had to seek help, because she couldn't deal with her daughter's death and some other things.

Another one of my regular, now rich clients, Jodi, that I mentioned previously, had been trying to get her sister-in-law Violet, to come see me for quite sometime. Finally, Violet decided to call for an appointment. Jodi had told her often that she came to see me monthly. It wasn't just to see what was in her future, but just coming to talk to me lifted her spirits and gave her hope for the things to come.

On Violet's first visit, she told me she now understood what Jodi meant, and she didn't know why she had waited so long to make it here. When she first came to see me, she was feeling quite depressed, but after the reading, she felt she had something to smile about. She told me that between readings, when daily pressures would get to her, she would replay the tapes of her previous readings, and it would lift her spirits. I let her know I enjoyed being able to give her help, and that it gave me inner comfort. The first day that I sat down with Violet to do her reading, almost immediately after I began, there was a Spirit loved one that made his presence known. It was a young man of very deep color. He was so dark, that I could hardly make out his features. He also had short, curly hair. It was her son that had died just after birth, and she hadn't thought about him for quite sometime. He showed me a vision of himself, as a young man at the age he would be now, about nineteen. He said that, although she had not been thinking about him, he was still around her a lot. Violet said that he was a very dark color when he was born, and there was a very special closeness between them. Those were the things she remembered mostly about him. She definitely felt better knowing that he was around giving her help with her life. On another occasion, I was able to bring Violet's sister in that had recently passed over. She told me about a purple dress that was in the closet and the family was undecided about whether to let her wear it for her wake.

They did let her wear it, and she was very happy. Violet asked, "How did you know that?"

I said, "Because she told me."

She also said that your brother looked good in his blue suit. She could hardly believe that I was able to tell her the information without being there, and she was happy that her sister was around her with love and help.

More Spiritual events began to happen when I did a Psychic party for another lady named Janis. The guests seemed to enjoy themselves, and the information flowed freely. After I was done reading for all of the guests, I offered to do a Psychometry reading for Janis. The reading was a gift, in appreciation for having me there.

As I started the reading, I saw an Army cannon and some sort of a modern machine gun, in my vision. I asked her if she had known anyone in the military.

She said, "Yes, my brother."

I asked, "Was he a prisoner of war?" I see his wrist being chained together."

She said "Yes."

I saw something on his arm that looked like a big flower, and she said he had a tattoo on his arm. I described his appearance, and she agreed that I was correct. I got the initial, G, and the name James was very strong with it. Her brother's name was Gordy, and his best friend, whose name was James, had been killed during the war.

Janis used to write to James when he was alive, but hadn't thought of him in years. I told her it was time that she did, because he was the one that was giving her the message. I hope that when she saw her brother, she gave him the message, because I felt it was for him, also. James wanted them to know they were still in his heart and he was still around them with lots of love.

Chapter 28

One day, I was invited over to a friend's house. She was a client turned friend, and still is; her name is Liz. She and her daughter Lisa were two of my first clients. Liz told me that she and Lisa had heard Spirits in their house. It seemed to always happen when they were home alone. They heard noises in the kitchen that sounded like someone was moving dishes around on the table, and Liz had heard something moving around in the attic. Lisa had seen the vision of a man standing in her bedroom doorway. They never had reason to fear these incidents but they were curious, especially since Lisa was the only one that had any Spirit appear to her. I thought it could be because Lisa was more highly developed Psychically. I knew, the first time that I read for her, she had very strong Psychic ability.

I had never been in their house before, so Liz showed me around and I admired the beautiful woodwork throughout the old place. Her dog greeted me for several minutes and when Liz was showing me around upstairs, the dog came along. Lisa was in her bedroom and I peeked in to say hello. Liz and I were standing in the small hallway that led to the three bedrooms, as we chatted back and forth with Lisa. While we were standing there, Liz asked me if I could feel the presence that Lisa had seen and heard. She had no sooner mentioned it, than I got the goose-bumps that let me know when Spirit is around. I felt there was a man's presence and it was very strong, his room was the second door from Lisa's.

I had no way of knowing that was a room they did not use. The door was shut, and when she opened it, there was no heat in the room and it was very cold; I could feel his presence even stronger. Lisa said that was the room she had heard noises coming from. The Spirit showed me that he was a man of around fifty years old. He had brown hair, was average height, and on the thin side. When I gave the description, Lisa said that was what the man looked like that she had seen in her doorway. Liz asked if there was a name for him, and the name George came to me. I shrugged it off as being too common, but I did say that I got the letter G, and to my surprise, Lisa said George. When Liz asked her how she knew, she said it just came to her, even before I mentioned the initial G. I asked her if she could feel his presence also, and she shook her head yes. George made it clear that he meant them no harm and they could borrow the house, but to make no mistake that it belonged to him, and he was there to protect it. As I mentioned before, the dog had followed us upstairs and was lying near us in the hallway. I noticed that she perked up her ears and was looking as though she could see something that she was not sure she was comfortable with. Then she started making a noise that sounded sort of like a moan, and she acted like it was pleasurable but uncomfortable at the same time. We started laughing at the dog's reactions, and George informed me that he was petting the dog. Liz said her dog made those noises all the time. I told her, I didn't think George knew that he was in Spirit, and I wanted to try something. I faced George's room and told him that he needed to go find the light. I let him know his family and friends were there waiting for him and that was where he was supposed to be. I repeated again, "Go to the light." It was as though he was turning around in the room, lost and looking for something. I could feel his eagerness to find what he was looking for.

I asked Lisa if she was getting any feelings and she said that she felt very anxious. After a couple minutes, George said, "I see it, but it's far away." He was walking toward the light and the closer he got, the more comfortable I felt. He said again, that he could see the light and his presence started fading away as I told him good-bye. He said he would be back from time to time to check on the house and make sure it was safe. I asked Lisa again, what she was feeling then, and she said, "Calm." The dog must have felt the same, because she started jumping up on me, and barking as though she was very happy; She acted like I had done something special. There have been a few other things that I have helped Liz and Lisa with. They always called me when they had articles that they couldn't find. Usually, I was able to tell them where the missing articles were located. Liz asked me for advice about selling her house, because she wanted to get rid of it and get an apartment for her and Lisa. I felt she would get what she was asking for it. I saw that it would sell in the Spring, because the sun was shining and it was cool outside; people were wearing light jackets, and school was still in session, as I could see children walking home from school. There were times that she got frustrated because the house did not sell as quickly as I had first thought it would. She even wanted to lower the price and take a loss to get rid of it, because it took a couple years before it sold. When she complained about it taking so long, I told her that in the Spirit World there is no such thing as time. I couldn't help the fact that I felt it would be soon, but when the time was right it would sell. I told her not to lower her price because she would get what she asked, if she would just hold out until it was supposed to sell. She signed her closing on a sunny cool day in the Spring-time, while school was still in progress, and she got the amount that she asked. She laughed as she said it was just as I had predicted.

Chapter 29

Laura is another one of my clients that I have made a lot of predictions for in the many years that she has been coming to see me. She has also been responsible for sending many other people to see me over the years. She always told me how good I was at reading for her. Each time she came back, she told me I was right about this or that bit of information, and how much help I have been to her. Although there have been many important predictions for Laura, there is one that sticks in my mind about the first time that she came to see me. When I sat down to do the reading for her, I tuned in with my Psychic vision and proceeded to tell her about what I had seen. I put my arm across the back of my chair and started shaking my hand a in a strange way. I told her that someone close to her shook his hand like that, and asked who it was. She said her father did, because he had Parkinson's disease. She was shocked that I was able to pick that up so clearly.

In another reading I saw problems with her husband's health. Many times after that when I read for her, I would get some upsetting feelings in the cards for him. I told her his health was not good and that he needed to moderate his actions because he was over indulging. She agreed that he wasn't well and later he went for some medical tests. She asked me what I felt about the results; I thought there was something definitely wrong. His test results came back showing that he had cirrhosis of the liver. He would really have to moderate his lifestyle, but I am sure God will send him lots of healing and help.

Laura is a very attractive and pleasant lady that always made me feel like I had a special gift. It's been a good feeling for me to be able to make a difference in her life. It's good to know that she had so much faith in me and for that reason, I strive to keep doing a better job. She also has been practicing Tarot and Astrology and wants to learn more on the subjects. She seems to have very good intuition, so I am sure she will do well.

Another story comes to mind about one of my clients, whose name is Lori. There was a lot of Spirit communication for her, from her parents and grandparents. Lori and her daughter Jada were two of my newer clients that have been coming to see me on a regular basis. Lori's first visit was a referral from Laura. The day that Lori came to see me for her first reading was filled with very strong energy from the Spirit World. When she sat down across from me, I could feel the goose-bumps going up my arms, but it was much stronger than it sometimes is with other visitors.   When I started the reading, an older lady came into my vision, with a lot of love and protection for Lori. With the information she gave, Lori knew right away that it was her grandmother who was present. She gave me the letter, R. Lori said that her grandmother's name was Ruby and that she was named after a precious stone. The old lady told me she had spent a lot of time alone, and she never left her room. She was ashamed of the way she looked because she was not able to keep her hair up as good as she would have liked to. Lori confirmed that all this was true, because she had been in a nursing home for years and she had been very fussy about her hair before she got sick.

She had been upset with Lori on her fifth birthday, because she had been showing off in her purple dress and spilled something on it. Lori confirmed that she did have a purple dress when she was around five years old that she adored.

121

Granny said there had been a lot of dissension between Lori and her brothers, but she was going to try and help them get closer. Lori agreed, that indeed, there had been problems with her three brothers. They had not been around much when their father needed them before he died. She had, and they were jealous of her because she and their father were close.

On another occasion when I read for Lori, I gave her some information about some money that she had coming from an insurance policy, and the amount was eight thousand dollars. Her father had just passed over and he came through. He wanted her to know there was more money that she had not found. It was in a blue envelope, or in something with a blue cover. He kept laughing while he was communicating, as though he was very happy. He said the reason he was so happy was because his left leg didn't hurt him anymore. Lori was amazed at his message, because he had always had a very painful left leg. Above all of his other aches and pains, he complained more about his leg before he died, because the pain became unbearable. Another time, her father tried to tell me that there was some property and a deed with his name on it, but Lori only knew of two pieces of property that he owned. He insisted there had been three houses, and it was not in this area. He said she would find out about it in due time. It would find it's way to her, but she needed to check and see if she could find any information about it. He left everything to Lori, and her brothers were jealous. They weren't cooperating and were being deceitful.

Lori's dad was around her daughter a lot, but Jada was afraid to let him communicate with her because she felt guilty for not paying much attention to him when he was alive. He was going to show her that he was not angry with her. He was going to turn her black desk light on, and she would know he was only there with love and comfort. In another reading, he was

122

still trying to help Lori find the policy that was supposed to go to her. He repeated, that he told her he had an eight thousand dollar policy. She had forgotten all about it until he reminded her. She couldn't believe she had forgotten him telling her something that was so important. It all came back to her when her memory was refreshed. He kept saying the word store, and he got the policy when he was with her mother. He spoke about a dark colored chest of drawers where he had taped a blue paper or envelope, and a cream colored envelope under one of the drawers. He showed me a special ring that was supposed to go to Jada. Lori confirmed that the chest of drawers her brother took was a dark brown color and the ring probably was the one that had a train on it. Her dad had belonged to a model train club. He said her middle brother that lives in this area had what she was looking for. After I gave her the message, she went and asked her brother if there was anything hidden underneath a drawer of the chest, and he said no. He also said she hadn't given him the ring that was supposed to go to her daughter. She had no doubt that he had the ring, because she remembered giving it to him. Her father seemed very upset that his sons were trying to keep their sister from having the money that was intended for her. Somehow he was going to see that she found the policy, along with the deed. He kept repeating that her brother was trying to cheat her, and it was very upsetting to think his son could do this. There was one reading for Lori that was strange in comparison to the other ones I had done, in the way Spirit came through. Every time she had been here, her Spirit Helpers were around her very strong. I never knew who to expect, until they started giving messages for her, and then they would tell me who they were. They always found a way to let her know if it was her mother, father, grandmother, or grandfather. I felt they had a very strong love for Lori, to be able to come in so easily. She seemed to have a good amount of Psychic ability, which could also be why they were around her so much. I was getting ready to close down, and as I did, I found myself thinking that was the first time I had read for Lori without her family being here. Usually, when I do a reading, Spirit comes through at the beginning, or early in the reading, to let who I am reading for know they are around. Then, they help with some of the information that I am supposed to pass on to their loved one. I guess, they heard my thought, because her Father came in strong and clear. He began telling me to inform Lori that he was still very upset and angry with her brother that lived near here. This was an added message in connection to one of the previous messages he had given her. He said the brother near here, knew about the insurance policy, and the other brother in Texas knew about the house or property. He couldn't believe they kept treating her that way. He was really going to be working on the brother that lived near here, and that he would unknowingly pass on the information to Lori when he was drunk. I asked Lori if her brother had a drinking problem, and she said, "Yes, sort of."

I could tell that her father was very upset, because when he first began to communicate with me, tears came to my eyes uncontrollably. I had the usual goose-bumps along with the tears. I asked Lori if her Father was sensitive and she said he had become so before he died. It was as though, along with the anger he felt for his son, he also felt hurt that they would be so dishonest. As he was talking, I had so many tears come to my eyes and I wiped them so much, I had to repair my eye make up when I was finished with the reading. I told Lori, I didn't mind him paying her a visit through me, but sending his sensitive feelings was something that I had problems with. It makes me show a sensitive side that I don't like to do, because sitting there with tears flowing as I was doing a reading must have looked like I was weird. But she also had tears flowing, so, I guess both of us made a strange looking sight.

After he stopped the tears, he started kidding around with her. He mentioned a stupid brown pair of pants that he hated, and she always picked them out for him to wear. They were baggy and ugly, but for some reason she always wanted him to wear them, like they were the only ones he had. He said something about a yellow shirt that he didn't like, and jokingly said she had bad taste in picking out clothes. She agreed, there had been a pair of brown pants that were baggy, and she always seemed to have picked them out for him to wear. She didn't understand about the yellow shirt, at that time. Later, she remembered that she had bought him a yellow pullover shirt for his birthday. She thought that he would look good in yellow and she got him the pullover, while knowing he only liked button-up shirts. She realized then, why he made the comment about not liking the yellow shirt. He seemed to like to pick on her in a loving way. She admitted that he always joked with her when she was younger and she would always fall for it, because she never knew when he was joking or being serious.

He showed me that his wife was quiet and stayed in the background when he was around. Lori agreed with his statement. He wanted to tell her that her daughter wore a pair of shoes that were old and they leaked, so her feet were getting wet. He wanted her to throw them away because he did not want her to catch a cold. He went on and on about the shoes, and said they had to go. Lori agreed that her daughter had a pair of old sneakers that she wore all the time. They did leak, and though she had a new pair, she wouldn't get rid of the old ones. He was worried about Jada, and he was going to start helping her. He was going to send someone to replace her Dad, so she does not feel so alone. (Lori is divorced, and Jada doesn't have much contact with her father.)

Lori's dad said he didn't understand why Jada was so afraid all the time, because he was nothing to be afraid of, and when he was around nothing was going to hurt her. Lori said the reason her daughter was afraid of Grandpa, was because of a couple of things she said to him before he died. Now, she had feelings of guilt for her previous behavior and she thought he was angry with her. He wanted her to know he had forgotten all of that and it was time for her to forget it also. It was also time for her to start spending more time in her room again; he described it as a rosy pink color. She would feel more calm and more secure in it because he was going to give her the strength to be more independent and not so afraid. Lori said that Jada hadn't slept in her room since Grandpa died, because her guilt had made her afraid. Lori also said that Jada had panic attacks and she is afraid of many things.

Lori's dad was quite the talker. Finally, I asked the old man if he was finished, and I had to tell him to be on his way. He was offended that I told him to leave, but when I jokingly told him I had things to do, he seemed satisfied and left. It had been a nice visit. I was amazed each time, how easy it was for him to come through, because I have never had anyone pop in to give messages repeatedly as he did. I suppose the reason was all the love that he had for them, and love was what made the barrier easier to cross. The visits from him brought much comfort to Lori and Jada; that is what my job is all about.

126

Chapter 30

I have had many Psychic experiences with Nina that I would like to mention. She is another client turned friend, and we have shared some very interesting Spiritual moments together. She is also a Psychic, and therefore, I could never understand why she came to see me. She would come for a reading periodically, so I suppose I gave her insight that she couldn't pick up for herself. After we became better acquainted, we would usually exchange readings.

I recall the first time I read for her. I was concerned about her ex-husband and the way he treated their daughter. It was one of the most disturbing impressions I have ever received. At first, bringing it up was hard for me, because I was afraid I could be wrong, but the feelings were so strong that I knew she needed to be warned. I told her that I felt her ex-husband was sexually molesting her daughter, who was only about seven years old. She said she didn't think that could be true, but she would check into the matter. That was another time that I had mixed feelings about my abilities. When she came back on a different occasion and told me I had been right, I was very upset for the little girl. On the other hand, I was glad that Nina had taken the necessary steps to take her daughter away from that horrible situation.

I have found that the telephone is a good instrument for Nina and I to use to channel together. The current going through seems to make it easier for us to connect.

One night, back when I still lived at the apartment, she and I were talking about my Guide, Tawl Horse, who helps me with my readings. At the time she didn't know his name, so I asked her if she could pick up what it was and was amazed when she said, "His name is Tawl Horse." She began giving me more information about him. She was explaining what he looked like, and as she did, I could see him in my vision just as she was describing, even before her words were spoken. I was really impressed that we could tune into the same things so well. I didn't understand why Tawl Horse hadn't been communicating more directly with me, so I would know more about him. I knew he had been helping me with my development and readings for a long time, but I didn't know what he looked like. He told her he was mad because I had the tomahawk raised in war, and he doesn't like war. When I changed the tomahawk to peaceful position, he would be glad to talk to me more.

Nina had never been in my bedroom. Therefore, she didn't know that I had started a Native American collection that was hanging on the wall. I did have a tomahawk, and yes, it was raised as in war. I changed its position the next day, and that night he communicated with me. It was a wonderful experience to know more than just his name, and that he was around in the background helping me. He showed me what he looked like, where he lived, and told me that he loved to eat rabbit.

Nina and I have shared many more Spirit contacts since then. I hadn't talked to her for a while because she moved to a small town about forty five-minutes south of here. One day she called, and as we talked, she was telling me about a police case that she was helping with. Even before she asked, I started to zoom in on several things that she confirmed were absolutely correct. I could see some of the people and places thought to be involved. I think that if we spent more time together working on developing our abilities, we could really expand our gifts to greater lengths.

One day, I drove down to see Nina. It was the first time I had been down to see her since she moved. We had lunch and then we were doing a reading for each other when Jon, a cop friend of hers dropped by.

They had been investigating a murder that had been committed years before which had not been solved. The two of them had been out to the old mansion where it had taken place. They ran into some strange occurrences when they were there, and they had taken pictures of the deserted house. They showed me the pictures and as I was looking at them, I began getting some strange impressions. This was the same case that Nina and I had discussed previously. The impressions that I was receiving were the same ones that I had gotten before, only this time, I picked up more about the situation. There was a woman that seemed to stand out more than the rest. I described her with dark hair and about thirty-two to thirty-five years old. I also described the man that I felt was responsible, a family member in his early fifties.

The information that I gave Nina and Jon seemed to fit what they thought was correct. The cop was so impressed that he asked me to go over to the old house with them to see what we could come up with. I said, that I wanted to get back home before dark, but I would come down another time and go ghost-busting with them.

Chapter 31

It had been quite a summer as far as my health was concerned, it seemed as soon as I got one thing fixed, something else tore up. I had some surgery and it turned out well, but I had some complications afterwards. Because of that, I had to go to the hospital for some tests.

The nurse, whose name was Melinda, did part of the tests, and as she was preparing me for the part that she would be doing, my channeling ability tuned in. I saw the vision of an old lady, and she gave me the name Kathryn or Kathy. I asked the nurse if that was anyone she knew.
She said, "No."
I asked if she was sure.
She said, "Yes."

Well, the old lady wouldn't give up. She wanted me to ask her if there was anyone she could think of who knew an old woman that walked crooked because of a bad back. Melinda thought again, and said, "Oh yes, that's my sister-in-law's name." That was her aunt, and they were very close. I felt the old lady around her very much, watching over her. I asked if she knew her and she said she did. They had spent much time together talking about many different things. The old lady was showing me a greeting card with pastel flowers on it. Melinda said she collects cards, and the old lady always got her an Easter card with flowers on it. The one that she was talking about had something funny on it. She wanted Melinda to find it because there was a special message in it that she needed to know.

There was something funny about the way the old lady dressed, and she didn't care if she wore stripes or squares together, as long as they were clean. Melinda agreed that she did dress differently, because her clothes never matched. The old lady just kept going on and on with her messages until I politely told her to be on her way, because we had things to do. Melinda seemed to enjoy her visit. I was the first Psychic that she had ever had contact with.

Later, when the Doctor came in to perform his part of the test, he asked me if I would read his mind. I informed him that I didn't read minds, and asked who had been talking to him. He jokingly said he would never tell. (Melinda had told him about her visit.) When he was done with the test, he asked again, if I would read his mind. I said, when I felt better, I would tape a reading for him. I taped the reading and dropped it off at his office, he reported to my primary care physician that I was a very interesting lady.

I also taped a reading for my surgeon and gave it to him when I went in for my checkup. He said he was afraid to listen to it. I told him that I couldn't understand how he was able to cut into peoples insides, and was afraid of a little Psychic advice. The reading showed that he was very Psychic. I was not surprised when he told me he was a Pisces, which is said to be one of the most Psychic signs. He told me his parents were gifted Psychically, and he seemed to be very proud of the fact.

Chapter 32

While I was still recovering, I had another strange experience happen. I had been over visiting with my sisters, and it had just gotten dark outside. I was very tired when I got home but it was too early to go to bed for the night, so I decided to take a little nap. I went into the bedroom, and turned on the air conditioner. As I was standing at the foot of the bed before I started to lie down, my eyes were drawn to look toward my pillow. When I did, I saw about three or four letters in a fluorescent green color. I don't like green, but it was such a soothing color, that I thought it was very beautiful. I somehow knew it was a message to tell me something, and I felt very comforted by what I had seen. The letter in the middle seemed to stand out more. I couldn't make out the others, but one looked like an M. I blinked my eyes and turned my head away and back again, and it was still there, then it faded away. It did not upset me at all. I turned the light on to see if there was anything there that could have shown up that way, and there wasn't. I didn't see it anymore after that.

I called my Psychic friend Nina, later that evening, and told her about the incident. I asked her what she thought, and she said it was news and love from Heaven. When she said that, I thought of my Mother. I asked Nina who it was, she laughed and said, "It's love from Mom." I knew when she was saying that, she was right, because the goose-bumps ran up my arms just as they always do when a message from the Spirit World comes through.

It was only a few days later, that I realized what that message was meant to say. It was Sunday, and I knew Boots, my "kitty companion" wasn't feeling well. It seemed, just as I started feeling stronger, she was getting weaker. When I had been feeling at my worst, and was lying on the couch, she couldn't get close enough to me. When I was lying down, she would stay near me more and more, and cuddle her face up next to my cheek as close as she could get. I recall thinking one day, as she cuddled near me, that it seemed as though she was trying to take away my illness. Later, I came to believe that was exactly what she was doing. It was Sunday, I was feeling better, and had decided to go to church for the Pastor's 25 Th. anniversary. I was in the shower, thinking about Boots being sick, and my mother came to me and said she was going to help Boots. Ordinarily, I would have thought she meant help with healing. When the message came, I started crying as though I knew she meant Boots was dying. I couldn't stop crying, and was unable to make it to the celebration. As my tears fell, I kept petting her and telling her I loved her. I couldn't understand this crying thing, because it wasn't like me to cry over an animal. I realized over the next few days, that this non- animal person was much more attached to her cat than she realized.

Boots was fourteen and one half years old, and had been given to my daughter when she was just a kitten of six weeks old. A neighbor had found her by the railroad tracks and brought her home. I had promised Vicki that day, that I would get her a cat. I guess it was meant to be, because she went down the street and came back shortly and said, Les, a neighbor who lived two doors down had given her a kitty named Boots. As it turned out, she became closer to me than to my daughter. Boots was around me more, and I fed her and took care of her most of the time.

Vicki loved her, but she teased her too much. She would hold Boots and forcefully pet her. Boots didn't like that and would get mad growl at her.

The next day after my mother's message, Vicki and I took Boots to the Veterinarian. He had been treating her for several months for a blood disease, and said she was so bad, there was nothing more to be done for her. He suggested that we let him give her a shot to put her to sleep to keep her from suffering. I wanted to bring her home to die, but he said that wasn't a good idea. We agreed to let him give her the shot. That was one of the hardest things I have ever had to do. Vicki and I held her, and cried with her for a few minutes before she died. We stayed with her and I held her, while she was given the shot. Thank God, that it only took a second to take effect. We took a few minutes alone with her, and then brought her home to bury her in the backyard. Bob dug the grave, while Vicki and I found a box to put her in. Then, we wrapped her in her blanket and put her favorite toy in her paws. With tears in all our eyes, we put her to rest. It was a very sad thing to have to do. It was really strange, how the dogs, Megan and Rambo, and the other cat, Chester acted. Usually, if we were out back, the dogs would be near us begging for attention, but this time they stayed up by the pool and didn't come near. Chester came down and looked around for a minute and walked away, as if he understood what was going on. I really believe they knew what had taken place, because they just laid around quietly, for the rest of the evening. Vicki and I had teary moments for several days. Bob even had tears, but that didn't surprise me because he is very much an animal lover.

It was only two days after Boots died that she appeared to me for the first time, and it was a wonderful experience. I was doing a reading, and my eyes were drawn to the floor at my left and I saw a small shadow, for only a second.   She appeared in the spot where she used to walk up to me, to see what was going on when I was doing a reading. When I saw her, a smile came to my face and I was happier the rest of the day. After that first time, she reappeared on several occasions. I touched her cold nose, when I was in bed that same night. On another occasion, I could feel her lying between my feet in bed. A couple of times, I smelled her breath beside me. She had a very offensive breath odor before she left us.

Her presence has been around us very much. I asked Vicki if she could sense her and she told me that she felt her lying on the foot of her bed one night. She also felt her presence with her when she went to Bowling Green one night to visit her friends. She was driving the car, and Boots came to mind very strongly. She started sneezing really badly, like she always did when Boots was around her. Vicki said she had also seen her in the basement. The sadness doesn't seem quite as bad, when you can feel her near. Maybe, that is why she is around so much, just to let us know that all is well.

Chapter 33

I have been associating more with other people that are interested in metaphysics. A Psychic friend of mine whose name is Iris, introduced me to a nice lady named Patricia who is also Psychic. I have known Iris for several years, and she also reads Tarot cards. She and I exchange readings from time to time.

I also got to know a lady named Sue better at that time, partially because of Iris. I had known her for years but hadn't really been around her much until she, Iris, and I started doing things together. Sue is also a Medium, and she and I read for each other a few times.

Since Iris introduced me to Patricia, she and I have become very good friends. We have been doing things together, such as sharing some common interests, and reading for each other. She reads the crystals, and she is getting really good at it. When I met her, she was not very sure of her reading ability, but I encouraged her to work with the stones more and try to be more self-confident.

She has been practicing with them more and I can see a marked improvement in her ability and self-confidence in the short time I have known her. She tries to give me some credit for helping her but I don't deserve any of the credit because her gift was there all along. She just had to be reassured of that fact, and have the confidence to use it more as she was supposed to do for helping other people.

I have been trying to help her sort out some bad childhood memories that she had suppressed. She feels, I have been able to give her some valuable information through my Psychic impressions. It seems, that every time she would start to talk about her past, I would be able to tune into her mother's Spirit. Through communication with her mother, I gave Patricia information that was comforting and helpful to her. It all started on the first visit that I made to Patricia's house. I was sitting across from her and was listening to her tell about her mother. Part of the discussion was about problems that she had as a child. When she mentioned her mother, I asked if she had died, and she told me she had. Her mother came through and wanted Patricia to know she was sorry. She knew what had been going on but didn't stop it, now she wanted to make it up to her. She also showed up another time and apologized again. She said, she loved her and wanted to be around to watch over her. It seemed like it was really easy for her to get through. It could be because of the feelings of love she was projecting that kept her around Patricia very strong. She always kept saying she was sorry. Some details she gave to me were so precise, that Patricia knew it had to be information only her mother knew. With the contact I made with her mother, she gave details of people and situations that has helped Patricia put to rest some traumatic experiences of her past. She and I can channel well together, like Nina and I used to do. It amazed her, the first time that we tuned in and saw the same vision at the same time. We got together one evening and we were trying different reading techniques for each other. Patricia wanted to do a Psychometry reading for me by laying her hands on my shoulders. When she began the reading, both of us shut our eyes at the same time, and when we did she saw several things, including my Guide Tawl Horse. The thing that amazed her, was what we both saw and described at the same time. It was a huge, beautiful, turquoise wave that appeared in our view and washed over us. It was a warm, wonderful, bright, and calming bluish green color. It had such great splendor that when we opened our eyes, everything else in our view seemed drab in comparison. It was a wonderful Spiritual experience for both of us. Patricia said she had never had such a Psychic experience with any other person before. I told her, I had similar impressions with another friend. Another great experience happened between us, one night. I was over at her house for a get-together with some other Metaphysical friends, and I had a vision for Patricia. I explained about a very old woman named Grandma Josephine that was by her side, helping her. She had wrinkles and long frizzy white hair. Later, when Patricia and I were alone, I had her to sit and meditate with me so she could see the old lady. She was able to describe the same vision that I had seen earlier, and again it was a wonderful Spiritual experience for us.

About a month later, Patricia told me she was making something that she wanted me to see. She is very creative at working with clay. I went over and when she showed me the old woman that she had made with clay, I was amazed to see that it looked just like my vision of Grandma Josephine. It is a beautiful piece of art that is so special it's hard to explain, because the doll was so unique and done in such great detail. I felt I had helped to give birth to her Guide that had been helping her, but had not been able to get Patricia to recognize her. She agreed that was the case, because she had seen the old woman before in her mirror, but was frightened because she didn't know who she was. I was so impressed with her doll that she offered to do my guide for me, and I gladly accepted. One night, she came over and said that she and I needed to meditate and ask my guide's permission to make a doll that looked like him. We sat down, and I called in Tawl Horse. When he came through, he brought along other Indians with him. It appeared they were having a

138

celebration of some sort. He showed me a young woman that I took to be his sister, an old man, and someone with many white feathers around him. I told Patricia that he could be White Feather, whom I had brought in sometime back for Bruce. It seemed like they were showing themselves so they could have a doll made in their likeness. Tawl Horse was doing a pretty nifty dance around a fire, and was really trying to show off his wares, so to speak. Patricia was impressed with his dance when she saw him. He didn't show a close up of his face. When she asked him to show her more clearly what he looked like, she got a weird feeling in her arms and hands and he told her that he would be in her hands when she started working with the clay. It only took her a few days to make him. She said that when she started his face with the clay, it seemed to take shape without any effort. She called me a couple of nights after she had been working on him, and ask if he had a scar over his left eye, because that was how it turned out. When she was talking about his scar, Tawl Horse started communicating with me, and said something about his left hand and it matches. I thought he meant he had a scar on his left hand to match the one on his left eye, and they were from the same incident. I told Patricia that he was talking about his hand, but I wasn't going to tell her what he said until she was done with him, because I wanted to see if he got the message through to her. When she brought him to me, it was uncanny how life like his features were. I was so impressed with her work with the dolls that I told her she should market them. I looked at his left hand and didn't see anything wrong with it. I told Patricia that he was talking about his left hand matching, and I thought he meant the scar. She said she goofed up and made two left hands and had to redo them. She kept trying to put it on and it didn't look right and realized they were both left hands. She had to make another one to get them to match. He kept telling her that his little finger on his left hand was chopped off, but she thought it couldn't be true; so she just made it shorter instead.

Something really strange happened the next day when I started to show him to my husband; I picked him up off the chair that he was on in my office, and when I did, I heard something drop on to the floor but didn't notice what it was. I went into the kitchen and showed him to Bob and was discussing all of the fine details that Patricia had put into his face. I picked up his hands and said, even his hands are detailed as well; when I lifted his left hand and was showing it to Bob, I realized that my Guide had lost his little finger. It looked like it had been chopped off above his second knuckle, and the break was completely even. That was what I had heard fall when I picked him up. He had been sitting in the same spot since I had put him there the night before. "Go figure." It's time to say "de de, de de." I told Patricia that things like this could really make you think you are crazy, if you didn't know you were at least halfway sane. She said the fact that it seems crazy is well worth the Spiritual excitement. She agreed that we have had some pretty strange Spiritual experiences. It seems that Patricia and I bring out each other's abilities. Hopefully, as time goes by, we can work with this energy and learn how to use it more to benefit both of us on our path of development. I am always open to learning new information that will help me grow Spiritually. She wants to learn the Tarot, so I gave her a beautiful deck of Tarot cards for her birthday. When I saw the deck, I knew they were made for her. She asked if I would teach her how to read them, and I told her I would be glad to. As time goes by, I realize Patricia is a very good and helpful friend that I can count on. I feel she is the friend that was sent to replace Mona and Geri, since they are not living here. Some of the loneliness that I felt for them is gone now.

Chapter 34

We added a new member to the family, and his name is Casper. He is a stray cat that came to the window and wanted in. He had appeared a few weeks before, and stayed outside all night meowing to get in. I wouldn't let him in because Bob's cat, Chester was hissing and growling at him.

To be honest, I wasn't ready to get attached to another cat, yet. Vicki had asked if we could get another cat, so we wouldn't miss Boots so much. I asked Bob if we could get a cat and he didn't say anything, which meant yes. It had only been a couple of days since I had asked him about getting a cat when the gray kitten reappeared at the door.

I had gone to run some errands, and when I got home, Bob told me the kitten had been here trying to get in. He brought it in and fed it, and put it back outside. He said it acted as though it was starving, and that was all I needed to hear. I walked out back, and yelled, "Kitty," but heard no response.

It was snowing very hard outside, so I came back inside, and as I shut the door, I heard a meow. I went outside again, and he was sitting on top of our privacy fence. He wanted down, but Chester had him treed up there. I asked Bob to go out and get him for me. The kitten came in, and ate like he hadn't eaten in ages. He settled in like he belonged here. He was very loving, for a stray cat. It was as though he had been away, but had come back again and felt very much at home here. He didn't even try to get out to go home, if he had one.

I told Vicki the first night he came that his face reminded me of Boots. Casper was more gray than she was, but he looked so much like her sometimes I found it hard, and still do, not think he is her. I felt she sent him here to replace her. He followed me around and he loved to be down in my office, just as she did. He also liked to lie in my chair that I sat in to do readings, which was one of Boots' favorite places to lie down.

The night we took him in, I brought him down to the TV-bar room, and Vicki took to him right away. I left him with her for awhile, and when I came back down later, she had been crying. When I asked her what was wrong, she said he reminded her of Boots and how much she missed her. She and I have come to the conclusion that Boots sent him to take away some of our sadness and loneliness from missing her.

The way we got his name wasn't easy. We thought of several names, but we didn't like what each other liked. After a few days, Bob was being sarcastic, and said, "I'm surprised, you haven't named him Casper." I said, "That's it!" All of us have really taken to him, even the dogs, but Chester didn't like his turf being invaded. He liked to stalk the new member of the household.

Chapter 35

It was around that time that my daughter decided to move down to Bowling Green to live and roommate with friends. She said it was time for her to be more on her own, and I guess she was right.

It was quite an adjustment for me, to get used to not having her around. I would have missed her even more, if I had not been already used to her living away from home when she was at college.

I am hoping that this will be a brief stepping stone until she can move to a larger city and pursue her career. Since she moved down there, she has gotten a new job at a Bridal shop. She has been able to use some of her degree, since the job has many duties, including assistant manager, buyer, and seamstress. Hopefully, it will give her enough experience to eventually move on to design clothes for the rich and famous.

She took a trip out to the Los Angeles area to visit friends. She liked being out there and is moving there soon. That might be where she will become successful. In my readings for her, I see great success in her future and it looks like out West is where it will happen for her. Hopefully, North Hollywood, since that is where she is moving to.

Since she moved to Bowling Green, she has had a couple of different apartments. She was living with some friends, but they moved to Cleveland and now her roommate's name is Lydia. They had a nice apartment that was very small and homey, but decided when their lease was up to get a larger place so they wouldn't feel so cramped.

I have a story to tell about their new apartment, and a visitor that they had. A few days after they moved in, I asked Vicki how she liked her new place and she told me she thought someone was there. I went down a few days later and when I walked into her bedroom, I definitely could feel a presence. It was stronger in her room, but was also there in Lydia's room. It was weird that I could only feel the heavy feeling on the side of the house where the bedrooms were located and not the other rooms. I felt it was a young man who was about twenty years old and had dark hair, but was not there to do harm. Vicki and Lydia both told me they could feel the presence at night when they were going to sleep and it felt like he was watching them. It made them so uneasy they could hardly fall asleep. Lydia thought it was an old man, and not the young one that I had envisioned.

I asked Vicki for some of the holy water that I gave her to keep on hand. While I sprinkled it through out the room, I said a prayer for God to send in the healing light of Christ and cleanse the room. I told the Spirit that was there to go to the light because he did not belong in the house. As soon as I did the cleansing, I could feel a lighter tone to Vicki's room and so could she. It must have worked, not only on her room but also on the whole place, because they have not had any problem sleeping since then.

I had some very Psychic impressions for Lydia the first time that Vicki introduced us. I had gone down to take Vicki out to dinner and she wanted me to meet Lydia. She seemed very pleasant, so I asked her to go eat with us and she accepted the invitation. We had a pleasant time getting acquainted as we enjoyed our meal. Lydia told me some things about herself including that she is the Psychic sign of Scorpio. After dinner, we went back to the apartment and Lydia showed me a picture of her mom who had passed over.

She started telling about her mother's death, and how she died. When she started telling me the details, her mom came through very strong, and was telling me what had really happened. I interrupted Lydia, and began shaking my head no, because her story was not correct. I took on her mother's feelings, which were very intense, and started telling Lydia what had really happened. Her Mom was with me, telling me what to say and how to put her feelings into the right words.

I told Lydia that a man nicknamed Smiley had murdered her mother. He had been romantically attracted to her and she refused his gestures. When she turned him down, he proceeded to leave. When he did, her mother decided to take a bath to relax, since the whole thing had been a trying ordeal. While she was relaxing in the tub, he came back in and held her under the water until she died.

Her mother said Smiley liked to drink wine and smoke pot. I saw a wine bottle, which was tall, skinny, darkly colored, and had writing on the label that would give her the information she needed to find out who this man was. I saw that he had scars on his face to this day, from where she scratched him. When Lydia told me they had cremated her, I gasped and said there was evidence under her fingernails. Her mother felt very frustrated, and said that Smiley had gotten away with murder, but he had ended up telling a friend named Jake about it. Jake was having a hard time dealing with the information, and feelings of guilt. She said, if Jake was ever found, he would tell everything that he knew about the crime. She also mentioned a woman named Jen, or Jennie, who was a friend that knew something about the crime, as well. She said that she loved Lydia, her sister, and brother. However, she felt closer to Lydia. She had a hard time relating to her son because he was always so quiet, but she loved him very much. She also said that Lydia's sister was the baby, and she was sorry she had not had much of a chance to have more of a relationship with her. Lydia hadn't previously told me any of the information that I had given her from her Mother. She was the oldest of the three children, her brother was second and her sister was the baby. They were all young when their mom died; her little brother got up in the morning and found their mother dead in the bath tub. Needless to say, that was very traumatic for a little boy to see. Lydia was fifteen years old at the time, and their aunt was kind enough to take on the responsibility of raising the children. Thank God for family ties.

Lydia confirmed much of the information that her mother wanted me to relay to her. Such as, there was a man that hung around by the name of Smiley. He was there the night her mother died, and he drank wine and probably smoked pot. She could remember the kind of wine that he drank and it was in a bottle like I described. She said she had always wondered if there was something strange about the way her mother died, and my information had helped her to understand it. She gave me a grateful hug as she thanked me for helping.

On another occasion, I gave her a bit of information that could be helpful to her. There was a short, dark haired woman, who was going to be helping with her career advancement. Lydia is an aspiring singer. Since I gave her the information, she met a lady named Mandy, and she is short, with dark hair. Mandy has fully financed a CD that features Lydia and her band with alternative music.

So hopefully, it will help her to get her career going in the right direction. She deserves a break, because she has not had an easy life. She is forever more asking me for Psychic information, especially about her love life. I try to help give her guidance as much as I can.

Chapter 36

After Vicki started sharing an apartment with Lydia, I decided to move my office up stairs, since I had an extra room. It was getting harder on my back to go up and down the basement steps so much. I had some older clients that had a hard time with the stairs, also. I fixed the office room up with all of my Native American articles. It definitely looks like a room that belongs to a Psychic.

Before Vicki moved out, I had started getting strange feelings when I was down in the basement. That started happening shortly before and after, I moved my reading room upstairs. The only explanation that I had, was around Christmas time, Darla, another one of my client friends, brought a male friend of hers over for a reading. According to the two of them, he was supposed to be Psychic. I could tell by talking to him, that he didn't know as much as he needed to know about being a Psychic. He was telling some stories about different bad Spirits that he had encountered, and I was getting really negative feelings with him. I believe he brought in a negative Spirit with him and it stayed here. It was after his visit that when I would be down in the basement by myself, I would feel that someone was watching me, and it made me nervous. It happened mostly in my reading room, and back by the laundry room. When I was in there doing laundry, I would have the urge to look out into the other room that was next to my office. It was a very uncomfortable feeling but I didn't mention it to anyone until later.

It was also, after I had moved my office upstairs, that I had a couple of strange dreams. The first dream was, that I walked over to the basement door and looked down at the bottom of the stairs and saw a young man. He appeared to be in his late twenties, with brown hair. He was beckoning to me to come down there. I could tell by the way he looked, that he had evil intentions. I told him to go away and I shut the door. I woke up really scared, because the dream was so vivid. The second dream was also vivid, but not as scary. The same young man was sitting in the bar room on the futon as I walked into the room. I was not as afraid this time, but when I woke up, I knew I had to do something to get rid of that Spirit and cleanse the basement.

I asked Patricia what she recommended that I use to cleanse it and she said to use sea salt. I decided to also use some of the Holy water that I keep on hand. So, as I sprinkled the sea salt and Holy water, I said a prayer and asked God to send in the white light of Christ to dispel any negative energy that was in my home. When the cleansing was finished, the energy in the basement felt better right away, and when I go down there now, I feel perfectly safe and secure.

After that, Vicki was here one day, and we were down in the basement visiting. I questioned her about any strange things happening while she was here. She began to say that around Christmas time, she started feeling like someone was watching her when she was in my office and in the laundry room. It made her uncomfortable, but she didn't say anything because she thought it was Boots. I explained that Boots wouldn't have made her feel afraid. Now, she and I both feel that all is well in the basement. As I mentioned before, Vicki definitely has Psychic ability. She is a lot like me when it comes to using her intuition, and therefore, she was able to pick up on the bad vibration.

Just after that situation with the negative feelings, I was lying in bed one night and was winding down before I went to sleep. I happened to look out into the hallway, and when I did, I saw beautiful little round splotches of white lights dancing on the walls. It was a very calming and enchanting sight to behold, and it continued for several minutes before disappearing.

I had a good feeling my Spirit Helpers were letting me know that all was well and they were giving me their protection. I was then able to fall off to sleep knowing that my home was filled with healing light. I saw the Spirit lights again in the same manner, a couple of other times after that, and again, I felt my Helpers were watching out for me. They were the same kind of lights that I have seen in Church many times before.

I told Darla sometime later, that I wasn't happy with the bad feelings I had from her friend. She agreed that something wasn't right with him, and she soon cut him out of her life. Darla was one of my regulars that had been coming to me since I started reading for the public. She does Astrology, but doesn't think she is as good at it as she really is. I have told her many times that she should read for other people, but she doesn't feel secure enough with her talent to do so. She has worked with Tarot cards some but she can't understand why she can't read them as I do.

One day during a reading for her, I had an interruption, and when I went back to the reading, I picked up where I had left off without skipping anything. She couldn't understand how I was able to do that. I thought everyone could, but she said she couldn't and neither could anyone else that she knew. She has given me a lot of confidence over the years. She has always told me that I am really good at what I do, and that it's a shame I don't use it as much as I should. She has often told me that I have told her many things that came about just as I predicted.

Her favorite prediction was about me telling her she was going to take a trip by water where she would be gambling. I felt the trip would be to Atlantic City, and soon. At the time, she had not planned to go anywhere, but a couple of weeks later some people that she worked with asked her to go to Atlantic City, and she went. She brings that incident up often, and gets excited when she says she still can't believe I was able to come up with the name of the place where she was going. It is always good to get positive feedback.

Chapter 37

One evening, I had a surprise call from Dee, who is one of my daughter's friends. She is a very smart and pleasant young lady. She asked me if they could interview me at the radio station where she works.

I told her that I felt honored that she had asked me, but why did she choose me? She grew up in a Metaphysical family, so she knows many other people in the field. Dee said the reason she chose me was that she trusted me and I am an upbeat person that enjoys my work.

The people at the station called me at home and interviewed me on the air by telephone. I was only supposed to be on the air for about fifteen minutes, but ended up being on for about fifty minutes. Before the interview was over, Ben, who was the host of the show, asked me to do a weekly show with him and Kim, his co-host. I agreed to do so, and started being on the morning show with Ben and Kim, as a call-in Psychic.

The employees at the radio station seemed very nice, and the listening audience seemed to enjoy my ability. Several employees at the station asked for a mini reading, and I obliged. They seemed pleased with their readings. One lady that I read for, found it quite interesting that her father came through from the other side. I described him and his temperament to her, and about an incident that had happened when she was thirteen years old. He wanted to make peace with her, and to let her know that he was sorry for being so mean to her when he was alive.

The reason he was coming through, was to let her know he had been changing his ways and that he loved her. She agreed, that he had been a nasty man when he was alive, and she was very glad he had changed. The visit from her father brought out a lot of sensitivity and tears, but she was glad that he had let her know he was around to help her when she needed it.

I did a full reading for Ben, who sometimes was a believer and sometimes not. Within a couple of days of the reading, he was astonished to know that some things I had seen had already come about. On one of the first shows I did, we were on the air, when Kim asked me if she was going to get a new car soon, and I told her it was going to be three months. She didn't like my answer, and said she couldn't wait that long because she needed one now. There would be two colors that she would choose from. They were black or red, but she would pick the red one. She would get a very good deal. On the next show, Kim told me she hated to prove me wrong but she was going out that day after the show to look at cars. I said, I had been known to be wrong a few times, but I still felt it would be three months before she got a car. On the following show, she said she had found the car that she wanted and was getting a great deal, but it had to be special ordered and would take at least two more months to arrive. She knew she wanted either black or red, but couldn't decide which color. She had the salesman toss a coin, and as a result of the toss, the red one was decided. Later she admitted that I was right after all, because it turned out to be three months, almost to the day. Kim kept bringing that prediction up from time to time as a testimonial to me.

The first day that I was on the show, Kim and I was talking after the show and Mark, the DJ who was on after us came in. I was pre-warned by Ben and Kim, that Mark was very intelligent but also very skeptical and analytical.

Mark joined in with our conversation about Psychic ability. He said he wasn't sure what he believed. However, he thought he had seen Spirit before, but he wasn't sure if he really had or if it was his imagination. He also thought he had precognitive dreams before that had come true, but he also questioned if they were just coincidence. He was the type of person that had to be shown exactly how things tick. Therefore, he was so busy analyzing everything that he was missing many good things in life. I told him that he should stop analyzing and start enjoying his wonderful gift that God had given him to make his life better. I also let him know that some things just can't be explained, and so you just have to accept it as such. The next week he came in after the show, and said he wanted to apologize, because Kim told him that he had been too hard on me. I told him, "No problem," because I was used to defending my beliefs. I let him know that I feel I can hold my own, and put anyone in their place if needed. Ben asked me to do a mini reading for Mark, and though I was a little hesitant because of his skepticism, I obliged anyway. During the reading, I told him some things that he didn't understand how I could know, but he was still skeptical anyway. It must have been a good reading after all because he made an appointment for a full reading.

When Mark came for the reading, I put all of my ability into it but giving him a good reading was extremely hard, because he was blocking me all the way. He would not give me any input even when I was on the right track, for fear of helping me in some way. It was probably the hardest reading that I had ever done. I felt I hadn't done a good job because it was like going up against a brick wall. He told me that he had a bad back and had tried several ways of treatment without any success. I offered to give him a healing to see if it would help.

He accepted the healing, and later, when I asked him how his back felt, he said it did feel better. He was still analyzing as he left, and I commented that I had been known to make believers out of the best skeptics. When I went to do the show the following week, I was talking to Ben before we went on the air, and he told me that I had made a believer out of Mark. He didn't think that could ever happen because he was so analytical and skeptical. I smiled to myself. Now Mark can't talk enough about Psychic subjects; and he admits that he believes in me. He asked me how to develop his ability more; and I told him to read as much as he could on the subject, then practice what he learned. As time went on, the show was doing well and Ben said the ratings were up. We had some very nice people who called and asked Psychic questions. They seemed to get much enjoyment from listening to the show. There were several people who called back later, and said the information that I had given them had come to pass. Ben asked several times if I would make worldly predictions on the air and I told him no. I didn't feel comfortable doing that because I felt better predicting on a more personal level. Although, around that time, I had a dream about the trial of the century, for the man who is nicknamed after that fresh squeezed juice. It was two weeks before the end of the trial that I dreamed he was found not guilty for the first part, but guilty for the second part. When I got up, I told my husband about the dream and asked if it made sense to him. He said it couldn't be that way. That dream was confusing to me until later, then it turned out to be just as I had dreamed. He was found not guilty for the murders, but found responsible at the civil trial.

Another worldly event that I had predicted was about the Gulf War. It was a couple weeks before it got really heated that I told my husband the exact day the President would send the troops over there to fight. I was shocked when I heard the President come on television and say they were going to send troops out before the day's end. I am always amazed at some of the exact information that my Guides give to me and extremely grateful for their help.

There is something that I would like to mention, that isn't a worldly prediction, but it is a feeling that I get. When I wake up in the mornings, I usually lie in bed for a few minutes before I get up. Sometimes as I am lying there, I get a very sad feeling for a couple of minutes. I put the feeling aside, and when I get up the feeling is gone, so I continue on with my day as usual. I have begun to realize that the bad feeling is a warning of something that will transpire that day. I finally sorted out what the feeling meant. When I started paying attention, I would always see on TV that day, the death of a famous personality.

Over the years I have read for many people from all over the world, including people from Russia, England, Barbados, and many states in our country, but I still preferred keeping my readings more personal and leave the worldly predictions to other people.

Chapter 38

I had a strange experience one Friday morning before I got out of bed to get ready to go do the show. I was lying in bed trying to wake up, when I saw a vision of Boots, and she was walking straight toward me, from the direction of her grave site.

It was very upsetting, because she looked ragged and sick like she did the day she died. I couldn't understand why she was showing me how she looked the day she died, rather than healthy and beautiful as I would have liked to remember her. I got ready and went to do the show, but was sad because of the dream. I kept thinking about Boots, and asking myself why she had shown me herself looking like she did on the day that she died.

On the way home from the station, I told myself that I should stop and buy a lottery ticket, but decided not to do so, because I wouldn't win anyway. Several times on the way home I debated whether or not to stop and buy a ticket, but came home without doing so.

That evening when the pick three lottery number came on the television screen, it was the month and day that Boots had died, IN ORDER. I should have paid attention to my thoughts, and sorted out the messages that she sent to me. I would have won a good sum of money if I had understood what she was trying to tell me, "straight and her death date."

Another morning, as I was waking, I saw a vision of Boots, and she was out on the back patio. She was sitting by the dogs' dishes, and they were in line in front of her, as though she was just sitting there trying to decide what one to pick to eat out of. Yet, I had the feeling that she ate already. She got up, turned her back to me as she walked down by the pool and out of sight.

Well of course, I couldn't understand what that meant until that evening, when I saw the "pick four" lottery number, and it was 8926, but not in order. Trying to understand Boots' message, I went out to look at the dog dishes, and there they were, all four of them. So then I realized, that she was telling me to play the pick four (four dishes), she ate already, (adding eight to her death date number) and back to back (walking away with her back to me.)

I would have won a good sum of money again, if I had understood what she was trying to tell me. I don't recall her trying to help me with numbers after that. I can't blame her for not wasting time again trying to get me to understand her messages, because I wasn't very smart with figuring them out until it was too late. Boots is always sending helpful messages to me, just as she sent Casper to replace her. He looks and acts more like her as time goes by. He does so many things just like she did, and that reminds me of her. Because of that, I have received many moments of warmth and laughs.

Shortly after that I left the radio station and soon following that, I decided to give up doing readings. I was having so many health problems that I needed a break. I was then able to do more writing as I felt up to it.

Chapter 39

About a year after Boots died, Bob's cat Chester got sick and died. He was only about seven years old when he suddenly got liver disease. His death was really upsetting for Bob. We had the same sort of burial for him as we did for Boots. Although, I liked him, I didn't miss him as much as I did my cat, and I have only had one vision of him.

About ten months after Chester died, I went to a junk yard to find a part for my car, and while I was there, I heard kittens meowing. I asked the man if I could see them, and he showed them to me. Right away, I saw a Tiger kitten that looked like Boots. I asked him if I could have her when she was weaned, and he said "Yes." I went back about five weeks later and picked her up. She was so tiny and cute, and she had a little gold spot by her heart that reminded me of the sun, so I named her Sunshine. The dogs, Megan and Rambo, and Casper took to her right away. She thinks Megan, the female dog is her mother; she lays between Megan's paws, and they lick each other. A few times, when she was a kitten, I caught her sucking on Megan's hair, looking for milk. Rambo, the male dog, tries to keep her in line because he is the dominate animal in the family. Now that Sunshine is older, she chases Casper, and he chases her. They romp and roll through the house. They really like each other, and it is a joy to watch them play. When they are running around, I laugh at them and call them crazy, and they show off that much more because they like to hear me laugh. Sunshine is a character, I call her my junk yard cat because sometimes when there's food around, she acts like a vulture. She is always getting into things, and she acts like a wild cat. She is really smart because she tries to answer the telephone when it rings and gets a plastic garbage bag out for me when she wants her litter tray scooped. She can also turn the door knob to open my door to my bedroom and office. She is looking more like Boots as she gets older, and I think that she looks like her twin. I tease her sometimes and call her Boots Jr. Before Sunshine came along, I thought Casper looked like Boots, but he clearly doesn't look as much like her as Sunshine does. She surely has brought lots of love into my life, and she is always doing something to make me laugh. She is very demanding of my attention, but she is a good companion just as Boots was. As time went on, the dogs started to get old, and we lost another one of the our family of pets. Rambo was almost thirteen years old when we had to have him put to sleep. His health was failing very badly. He had arthritis and a mass on his throat that caused him to suffer in the end. When he died, it was a relief to see him not suffer anymore. It was a very sad time for us, especially Megan, because he had been by her side all of their lives. Her health is starting to fail also, and I am hoping Bob won't allow her to suffer, as long as he did her brother. It is hard when you care so much for animals, because you don't want to loose them, but you don't want them to suffer either. It's like being between a rock and a hard place. We shed a lot of tears when we lost Rambo. Bob and I were really upset, because you can really get attached to an animal when you are around them all the time. Megan was really lonely for awhile and needing more attention. I think she still is adjusting to not having him around. It didn't take long for Rambo to appear for the first time after he passed. It was in the late evening and as I started running my bath, Megan gave a little bark like she usually does when she wants something. She was lying in the kitchen with her back to the dining room and hallway; when I asked her if she wanted out. She wouldn't get up, and when I asked her what she wanted, she looked over her shoulder toward the dining room. Since I didn't know what she wanted, I went about my business of running water in the whirlpool. She barked again, and we went through the same process again. I went back to what I was doing, and she did the same thing again. I told her to be quiet because I was going to take my bath. Keep in mind that was the most she had barked since Rambo died. I had just dimmed the lights and hopped into the whirlpool to relax, when I saw a shadow in the hallway by the bathroom. It frightened me at first, because I wasn't expecting it, but right away, it came to me that it was Rambo. It wasn't large enough to be a human Spirit, and it had the shape of a large dog. I could even see the darker color by his left eye, as he headed in the direction of the bedrooms. Megan quieted down after that, so I am sure she had seen the visitor. Later, before I went to bed, I was looking at the calendar, and when I saw the date, I realized, it was four weeks to the day since Rambo had left. I thought his appearance was a good four week anniversary surprise. It was an exciting feeling, to know that he had made it through to let us know that he was giving us help and healing.

One evening, I had a very strange experience happen with Sunshine that I was unable to explain. I decided to go down to the basement to exercise on the treadmill. It was late at night, and only myself and the animals were here, since Bob still worked the night shift. The room that the treadmill is in, is where I had my office before I moved it upstairs. When I went down, I looked for Sunshine. She was in the bar room under the futon, in one of her special hiding places where she sleeps. I said, "There you are," and then went in to start my walk. She followed me, but seemed a little startled at something. I was talking to her and she suddenly started to act weird. She seemed really nervous as she was looking at her food dish like she didn't know what it was, and was afraid to go near it. She kept sneaking around it, and wanting to check it out, but there was something about it that scared her. She then walked over by the wall, and was looking at the blanket that I had folded for her and Casper to lie on. She acted the same way with the blanket as she did with the dish. She stalked it in a scared sort of way for several minutes before she finally went near it. Then, she went back to the dish, and was still nervous until I told Boots to tell her it was okay. About two seconds later, Sunshine walked up to it and started eating as usual. It appeared that whatever had made her so uneasy, had abruptly stopped. By the way, the dish and the blanket used to belong to Boots, and the basement was a special place to her. The reason I sent the thought to Boots was, I felt it was she that Sunshine was seeing and she didn't know what to make of it. I could feel her presence, and I told Sunshine that Boots would not hurt her, because she looked just like her. I keep thinking that Sunshine is Boots' replacement, because she acts and looks more like Boots as time passes. The night before that incident happened, I had a strange dream about Boots, I don't know if there was a connection or not. I dreamed it was Boots' ninth birthday, and we were giving her a party. She was sitting at the party table, just as a child would, and I was standing behind her chair. She turned around and looked at me with an upset expression on her face because she did not like having to sit there for her party. I was able to feel her feelings of restriction and fear. That might have been because she was afraid of most people, especially strangers. I realized, shortly after that the dream had special significance concerning an important personal matter for me. The message was

161

very accurate as usual when I sorted it out. All of her dreams have given me some special messages. It still brings a smile to my face and a warm feeling to know that my little companion Boots is still around. It makes me feel good to know that she is here to give me help and healing.

I have grown to really love animals as I have gotten older and developed Spiritually and Psychically. They have become a very important part of my life. I think that is because not only are animals healing to be around, they also help me to be more sensitive. Because of that, I am more intuned Psychically, as they are. They surly have brought me many laughs, which in turn brings warmth and healing.

Ending Thought

I feel that what we all need in our lives are smiles on our faces and warm feelings in our hearts. If I were asked what I felt would cure the problems of the world, I would say, that if there was more love and laughter, it would be a much more pleasant place to live. I have had many wonderful experiences since I have acquired the ability to communicate with the Spirit World. I know there are people that don't believe Spirit communication is possible, but I truly believe that God has given me this honor. There is no way I could come up with some of the information that I do without the help of Spirit. Since I have found this gift, I feel closer to God and I am not afraid of the afterlife. I think it is the beginning of a whole new and beautiful existence that goes on forever. I wish, that in everyone's life, they could personally have at least one opportunity to receive a message from someone in Spirit, so they can experience what a wonderful feeling it can be. We all have Spirit Helpers around us at all times. They might be loved ones, or people that we have never known who have passed over and chosen to help us learn the lessons that we need to learn on this Earth. WE ARE NEVER ALONE, because they are always near, giving us guidance and helping us to make decisions.

When God feels we have learned all the lessons that we need to learn here, he makes it possible for us to go over to that special place and join the ones that helped us to progress and grow. Then, hopefully, we will be able to help people who need our guidance to learn the lessons they need to learn while they are on Earth. I hope, as you read about some of the lessons I've learned thus far, it will help you to accept your Spirit Helpers, so they can help you to learn and grow.

In writing this book and sharing some of the special experiences with my Spirit Helpers, I hope it will bring some laughs, warm feelings, and healing into your life.

Many Blessings...   163